THE ELEPHANT AND DHARMA

Lotus Zen

THE ELEPHANT AND DHARMA

42 Reflections inspired by Hindu thought

Copyright © 2023 - Avenet Edition

All rights reserved. No part of this publication may be reproduced, distributed or transmitted in any form or by any means, including photocopying, recording or other electronic or mechanical methods, without the prior written permission of the publisher, except in the case of brief quotations incorporated in reviews and certain other non-commercial uses permitted by copyright law. All references to historical events, real people or places may be real or used fictitiously to respect anonymity. Names, characters and places may be the product of the author's imagination.

Contents

Foreword	9
1. The Elephant and the Sage	12
2. The Peacock and the Sacred Fire	16
3. The Monsoon drops	20
4. Krishna and the Shepherd	24
5. The Lotus in the Mud	28
6. The Serpent and the Hermitage	32
7. The Banyan and its Shadows	36
8. The Yogi and the Bandit	40
9. The Tiger and the Monk	44
10. The Eagle and the Mantra	48
11. The Shiva Stones	52
12. The Dance of Parvati	56
13. The Chariot and Karma	60
14. Rama and the Old Bridge	64

15. The Monkey and the Illusion	68
16. The Antelope and Meditation	72
17. Saraswati's Mirror	76
18. Brahma's Bird	80
19. The Deer and the Mandala	84
20. The Vishnu Ladder	88
21. The Butterfly and the Vedas	92
22. Ganesha and the Honey Pot	96
23. The River and the Aatman	100
24. The Wind and Arjuna	104
25. The Swan and Advaita	108
26. Fire and Bhakti	112
27. The Desert and Moksha	116
28. The Squirrel and the Ramayana	120
29. The Turtle and Yoga	124
30. Heaven and Samsara	128

31. The Sun and Brahman	*132*
32. The Mountain and the Detachment	*136*
33. The Hare and the Maya	*140*
34. The Moon and the Rishi	*144*
35. Forest and Dharma	*148*
36. The Lake and Reflection	*152*
37. The Parrot and the Mantra	*156*
38. The Dolphin and the Vairagya	*160*
39. The Owl and the Night	*164*
40. Mangosteen and Essence	*168*
41. The Garland and the Atman	*172*
42. The Elephant and the Dharma	*176*
Conclusion	**181**
Thanks	*183*
Source Images	*185*

FOREWORD

At the heart of Hindu wisdom lies the notion of dharma, a profound principle that governs not only the order of the universe, but also the personal trajectory of each being. It's a concept that embraces ethics, duty, justice and each individual's own path in life. In "The Elephant and Dharma: 42 Reflections Inspired by Hindu Thought", we explore this golden thread of ancient wisdom through parables from nature, embodied in creatures and situations that reflect our own struggles and aspirations.

Like Gajendra, the majestic elephant whose story opens and closes this collection, each story here mirrors the human quest to find balance and a place in an ever-changing cosmos. These fables, emanating from the forests, mountains and rivers of India, from the stars that line our skies, to the silent depths of our own hearts, are reminders that every creature, every element, every thought has its definite place in the great order of things.

These stories are not mere narratives; they are teachings, meditations that invite reflection, discovery and inner enlightenment. As the wise Vidyadhar guides the elephant Gajendra towards a deeper understanding of his role in the forest, each chapter of this book aims to guide you towards a deeper understanding of your own dharma.

As you prepare to turn these pages, I invite you to open your heart to the lessons hidden in each story, to find the resonance between these ancient wisdoms and the rhythms of your daily life. May this book be for you a companion in the quest for balance, a source of comfort in moments of doubt, and a beacon of clarity in the sometimes-tumultuous ocean of existence.

We begin our journey with Gajendra, whose power and wisdom embody the eternal quest for harmony and understanding. May his majestic walk inspire your steps on the path of knowledge.

Welcome to a world where every step, every breath, every moment is a celebration of the dharma that unites us all.

Your opinion counts!

Once you've finished this book, share your review on Amazon.

Your feedback will be useful for future readers.

I look forward to seeing how this book has impacted you.

Thank you in advance for your contribution, and happy reading!

1. The Elephant and the Sage

The importance of patience

In the heart of India, where the dense jungle hugs the banks of sacred rivers, lived Garuda, a majestic but particularly impatient elephant. Everything always had to happen quickly for him, whether crossing the verdant plains or bathing in the gentle waters of the river. His constant haste often caused havoc, frightening other animals and eroding the paths he took.

One day, on one of his wild chases, Garuda knocked over a hut housing an ancient sage named Vishnudas. The old man, though shaken, emerged from his crushed dwelling with a peaceful countenance and no trace of anger. Intrigued by such serenity in the face of disaster, Garuda stopped, feeling guilty.

"O revered sage, I'm deeply sorry for the wrong I've caused you," Garuda exclaimed, humbly bowing his head.

Vishnudas, smiling tenderly, replied, "Destruction is often the fruit of impatience, majestic Garuda. But everything can be repaired with time and patience."

The sage's words echoed in Garuda's mind. He realized that his constant haste had brought him nothing but trouble. "Master, I wish to learn patience. May I stay by your side to understand this virtue?" he asked.

Vishnudas gladly accepted and offered Garuda a challenge. "For the next seven days, you'll have to help rebuild my hut, but on one condition: you mustn't rush. Every action, every movement, must be carried out with thought and care."

The challenge was far more difficult than Garuda had imagined. Each stone he placed, each branch he adjusted seemed to take an eternity. More than once, he was tempted to speed up the process, but Vishnudas' soothing gaze encouraged him to persevere.

As the days passed, Garuda began to perceive the world differently. He watched the butterflies dance slowly from flower to flower, the leaves fall gently from the trees, the clouds move gracefully across the sky. He realized that the world was full of subtle beauties that had escaped him because of his impatience.

On the seventh day, the hut was rebuilt, more beautiful and stronger than before. With tears in his eyes, Garuda thanked the sage. "Master Vishnudas, thanks to you, I've discovered the beauty of patience. I will no longer rush ahead without thinking, for I now know that haste masks the wonders of the world."

Vishnudas nodded approvingly. "Patience, Garuda, is not simply the act of waiting. It's the understanding that each moment has its own value. By embracing patience, you embrace the beauty of the universe."

Garuda, deeply transformed, took his leave of the sage with gratitude. From then on, he traversed the jungle not with haste, but with grace and admiration for every moment. And the legend of the impatient elephant who became the embodiment of patience spread throughout the jungle, inspiring generations of animals and humans alike.

The Wisdom of the Present Moment

Patience is much more than a passive virtue; it's a conscious openness to the natural rhythms of life.

The story of Garuda teaches us that impatience can blind us to the riches slowly unfolding around us. Each moment carries with it an infinite number of magnificent details, accessible only to those who venture to welcome them with tranquility. To embrace patience, then, is to embrace life itself, to recognize and appreciate the intrinsic value of each moment.

By integrating patience into our daily lives, we become active witnesses to the beauty hidden in slowness, and our existence is irrevocably enriched. Garuda, the impatient elephant, has become a symbol of transformation, reminding us that in calm and deliberation lies the key to a previously invisible world, revealed in all its splendor.

2. THE PEACOCK AND THE SACRED FIRE

Inner beauty versus appearance

In a lush valley bathed in India's soft light, a peacock named Mayura strode with visible arrogance. His gleaming feathers drew the admiration of all the forest's inhabitants. Mayura knew it, and his heart beat to the rhythm of the compliments he received every day for his outward magnificence.

Yet in this same valley lived a wise man who, day after day, fed a sacred fire, symbolizing wisdom and inner purity. Villagers came from far and wide to lay their offerings there and pray for a beauty that does not fade with time: that of the spirit.

One afternoon, as Mayura was parading, a child asked him, "Who is more beautiful, O wondrous peacock, you or the sacred fire that glows in the sage's hut?" Amused by a question that seemed so naive, Mayura spread his feathers in a flaming glow and replied, "Look around you, child. What beauty could surpass mine?"

Curiosity piqued, Mayura approached the sage's hut to see the fire that so fascinated people. The sage, sensing the peacock's presence, invited him to join the evening meditation. Mayura, strutting his stuff, accepted, convinced that even the fire would pale beside his splendor.

As night fell, a meditation began. The sage invited everyone to close their eyes and seek the light within. Mayura found the exercise ridiculous; after all, what could be brighter than him? But as silence settled in, something surprising happened. In spite of himself, Mayura closed his eyes and, for the first time, looked inside himself.

Then he saw her heart, which had neither the brilliance of her feathers nor their variety of colors. He understood that the inner beauty of which the sage spoke was a different light, a light that did not depend on compliments or admiring glances. It was a light of peace, goodness and truth, which could not be tarnished by time or circumstance.

Mayura opened his eyes, feathers less spread, and looked at the sacred fire burning steadily and gently. He realized that this fire, though not dazzling like his plumage, had a beauty all its own: it warmed souls, guided spirits and symbolized the eternal light of wisdom.

The peacock humbly approached the sage and asked how he could light this inner fire. With a gentle smile, the sage taught him the virtues of generosity, honesty and compassion. Mayura listened attentively and promised to seek the beauty that lies in the act of giving, not just in the act of receiving admiration.

And so the proud peacock began to dance, not to boast of his feathers, but to share the joy with those who watched him. And with each movement, a new feather seemed to grow in his heart, a feather of light, invisible to the eye but resplendent to the soul. Mayura had become the most beautiful peacock, not because of his appearance, but because of the inner flame he had learned to cherish and cultivate.

The Inalterable Radiance of the Soul

True beauty transcends appearance. Mayura the peacock, seduced by the shimmer of his feathers, discovered that a far more precious splendor burned within the sacred fire. This story reminds us that the light that emanates from within us, the light of our values and goodness, is the one that illuminates our path most durably.

The lure of compliments and the desire for admiration are fleeting, and often only feed our vanity. Mayura's lesson is a hymn to humility and the search for authenticity. The beauty of the spirit, unlike that of the body, does not wither with time, but grows richer with every act of generosity and every sincere word.

Finally, Mayura's evolution towards an appreciation of inner beauty reveals that the greatest gift we can offer the world is the example of a life lived with integrity and love. The transformation of the peacock illustrates that our greatest asset is the flame of wisdom and compassion we nurture and share with others.

3. The Monsoon drops

Unity is strength

In the pulsating heart of the monsoons, where heaven and earth meet in a liquid embrace, a single drop of water was born from the union of a cloud and a warm breeze. Her name was Bindu and, unlike her sisters who hurried to earth, she dreamed of becoming a river, traveling across plains and valleys, nurturing life and singing liquid melodies.

Bindu fell from the sky, swirling with a grace that only a raindrop can possess. She touched firm ground, penetrating the dry soil, and there she met other drops, also dreamy and ambitious. "Let's join together and form a stream," she proposed cheerfully. But the other drops scoffed at her desire. "We're just drops, Bindu, ephemeral travelers from one sky to another, nothing more."

Yet Bindu refused to give up on her dream. She traveled through cracks and rocks, gathering other drops around her, sharing her vision. Soon, a small band of water drops, animated by the promise of an existence greater than their own ephemerality, followed her.

Over time and through storms, Bindu and her companions coalesced and swelled, first forming a thin trickle of water that meandered hesitantly. As they advanced, the trickle grew in strength and confidence, fed by the relentless flow of monsoons. The trickle became a stream, the stream a river, and the river widened into a mighty, majestic current.

The Bindu River, as it soon became known, flowed through the villages, bringing life and prosperity. Peasants worshipped it like a goddess, children played in its gentle waves, and animals came to quench their thirst at its welcoming banks.

One day, a wise man came to meditate on its banks. He spoke to the river: "Bindu, your dream was pure and noble. But do you know the source of your strength?" The river murmured with the wisdom of all the drops that formed it.

"It's unity," she replied, "Alone, I was just one drop among many, but together, we created a flow of life."

The sage nodded and smiled: "This is dharma, the universal law. Just as drops of water unite to form a river, so souls unite in the ocean of existence. Alone, you are a drop; united, you are an infinity."

Bindu, the river, flowed on for many more years, through seasons and ages, singing the same refrain - a hymn to unity, common strength, and the beauty of shared life. She taught all those who listened that even the smallest drop of water can become an essential part of a grand whole, as long as it believes in the strength of union and the power of mutual aid.

Thus Bindu remained, even after its waters had merged with the ocean, a symbol of what unity can achieve and a reminder that even the smallest dreams can lead to great destinies, if harmony and collaboration are sought.

The Power of the Union

Each drop of water, like a single aspiration, may seem insignificant when isolated, but together they have the power to sculpt landscapes and nurture life. Bindu's story inspires us to recognize the value and potential of each individual, and even more, the collective force that emanates from the unity of these individuals.

Bindu's ambition to become a river, despite ridicule, is a vibrant testament to perseverance and faith in a shared vision. It teaches us that when we channel our efforts towards a common goal, the barriers of ephemerality crumble, giving way to the emergence of a transformative force.

The journey of the Bindu River, which became a vital axis for the communities it passed through, illustrates that by uniting our talents, our dreams and our actions, we can generate a lasting impact. It is in the synergy of small efforts that lies the capacity to create change and realize the most grandiose aspirations.

4. Krishna and the Shepherd

The simplicity of life

In the lush valley of Vrindavan, where the murmur of rivers and the song of peacocks merge into an eternal melody, lived a shepherd named Madhav. His days were simple, punctuated by the breath of the wind and the slow steps of his goats. Yet hidden in his simple heart was a longing for a life richer and more ornate than the one he led.

One day, as the sun began its descent, tinting the sky orange and pink, Madhav saw a figure approaching who seemed to be dancing to the rhythm of nature. It was Krishna, the blue-skinned god, coming in the guise of a young cow, carrying a flute on his lips and a mischievous smile in his eyes.

Intrigued and oblivious to the divinity before him, Madhav addressed the stranger. "O young cow, your bearing is cheerful, your gait light, but tell me, do you not desire more than this simplicity? Don't you dream of palaces and riches, jewels and silks?"

Krishna smiled and, putting down his flute, replied, "Madhav, simplicity is the cradle of joy. Palaces are golden prisons and riches are chains that shackle the soul."

Eager to understand this strange philosophy, Madhav invited the cow to share his frugal meal. Together, they ate rice and vegetables, sitting on the nourishing earth. "Look around you, Madhav," Krishna began. "Trees don't require gold to grow, nor rivers jewels to flow. They simply exist, giving and receiving with balance. That is all wisdom."

As the shepherd listened, absorbed in Krishna's words, a soft light began to emanate from the cow, and the veil of mortality seemed to lift from her face. Madhav then realized with whom he was speaking, and fell at his feet, moved and ashamed of his material desires.

Krishna, the almighty, raised Madhav and spoke to him tenderly: "Don't weep for the desires of your heart, for it's human to have them. But learn to find joy in simplicity, to embrace life as it comes, with all it offers and all it doesn't give."

As a blessing, Krishna offered Madhav his flute, telling him, "When you play, remember that the purest music comes from within, not from external adornments."

Years passed, and Madhav, the shepherd, became known for his wisdom and his melodious flute. He no longer aspired to material riches, for he had discovered a far more precious treasure: the inner peace and serenity of a simple life, teachings he had received from the god Krishna himself.

And so, in the valley of Vrindavan, Madhav's music resounded, not as a reminder of what might be, but as a celebration of all that is, simple and unpretentious, yet brimming with the purity and wisdom of Dharma.

Harmony in Simplicity

Madhav, the shepherd of Vrindavan, learns from his encounter with Krishna that material desires, though human, are not the essence of fulfillment. This lesson resonates deeply in a world where outer abundance is often confused with inner happiness. The simple yet powerful truth is revealed: true joy comes from appreciating the most fundamental elements of life.

Krishna, in his divine wisdom, illuminates the fact that nature itself is free from the greed of ornaments; it thrives in its purest state, asking for nothing in return. This wisdom is a valuable guide for Madhav, and by extension, for us all, inviting us to rethink the value of what we seek, and to rediscover beauty in everyday life.

Madhav's transformation from a seeker of material wealth to a sage celebrated for his music and inner peace is a testament to the liberating power of simplicity. His story reminds us that the purest music, like the most fulfilling life, emanates not from possessions, but from harmony with our true essence and environment.

5. The Lotus in the Mud

Purity in adversity

In the tranquil garden of an old temple, where silence was often broken only by the chanting of prayers, a young lotus was about to be born, buried in the mud of a peaceful pond. His name was Kairav, and even in the darkness of the mud, he carried within him an inner light, a purity destined to pierce the veils of dark water.

As Kairav grew, he saw other plants withering around him, dulled by mud, absorbing the shadow of their surroundings. But Kairav was different. He had heard the ancients speak of the true nature of the lotus, which, despite the murky waters, always emerged pure and resplendent.

As Kairav finally broke through the surface, unfurling his petals in the sunlight, he was confronted by the constant splashing of mud. Creatures wandered about, stones fell into the pond, disturbing the water and leaving new layers of sediment on his silky petals. Yet Kairav used every drop of water to clean and rinse its surface, letting the mud flow, holding nothing back.

Visitors to the temple marveled at Kairav's beauty, its unaltered radiance despite the mud that surrounded it. They often came to sit by the pond, meditating on the lotus image, trying to understand how they too could remain pure in the midst of life's adversities.

One morning, as dawn gently brushed the petals of Kairav, the temple priest approached the pond, his feet leaving wet footprints on the dry earth. He crouched beside Kairav, his hands clasped in prayer, and whispered: "O Kairav, you are living proof that one can be in the world without being of the world. Tell me, what's your secret?"

Kairav, through the grace bestowed upon him, found a way to communicate with the old priest. "Purity is not a resistance to mud, but an acceptance of its presence. I don't fight it, I recognize its role in my growth. It nourishes me, but does not define me. My nature is to remain pure, in spite of it."

Kairav's words resonated with the wisdom of ancient scripture, teaching all who came seeking answers that purity is not a battle against dirt, but a constant affirmation of one's own essence. The mud of the pond is the world, with its sorrows and troubles, and the lotus is the soul, emerging and immaculate, finding its strength in its own unaltered nature.

And so Kairav lived, through the seasons, through the rains and the bright sun, always pure, always serene. His story became a legend in the temple, a living symbol of purity in adversity, reminding those who seek the Dharma that true purity comes from within, never tainted, no matter how deep the mud.

The Serenity of the Unshakable Soul

Kairav, the lotus that transcends the mud of its native pond, teaches us an essential truth: the purity and serenity of the soul are not determined by external circumstances, but by inner strength and clarity. So, no matter what the challenges or adversities, our essence can remain immaculate if we choose to. It's an invitation to resilience and grace under pressure.

Mud, a metaphor for life's trials and defilements, fails to mar Kairav's splendor, for he understands that it is both part of his existence and distinct from his true identity. This distinction is vital for anyone seeking to remain true to their principles despite hardship. Kairav teaches us that purity is an expression of our deepest nature, which does not yield to external pollution.

The lotus in the mud thus becomes a symbol of our ability to thrive despite difficulties, to maintain our integrity in all circumstances. Kairav illustrates the ideal of a life lived with dignity and authenticity, where purity is an untouchable state of being, fueled by personal conviction and not by the environment.

6. The Serpent and the Hermitage

Overcoming prejudice

In a lush forest where the ground was strewn with ancient leaves and the trees whispered the secrets of the world, there lived a snake named Naga. His reputation preceded him, like a sinister wind heralding a storm. The local villagers, guided by terrifying tales, feared Naga, which condemned him to deep solitude in the dark recesses of the hermitage where he had made his home.

Naga, however, was not the malevolent creature the legends portrayed him to be. He was wise and peaceful, often meditating on the nature of existence, feeding on the knowledge offered by the sacred texts forgotten in the hermitage. He longed for companionship and acceptance, but the fear he inspired created an invisible barrier around him more impenetrable than the thickest walls.

One day, a holy man came to stay in the hermitage, a wise man who had traveled through distant lands and carried with him a light of acceptance and understanding. He met Naga and, instead of retreating in fear, he sat down beside him and shared his food.

"Why aren't you afraid of me?" asked Naga, her voice a soft hiss in the quiet of the forest.

"Fear," replied the wise man, "is often the fruit of nourished ignorance. You are not the creature the stories tell. You simply are, and that deserves respect and consideration."

The sage's words touched Naga to the very depths of his being. Together, they spent days, weeks and months discussing philosophy, dharma and the nature of reality. The sage taught Naga that it wasn't up to him to change the nature of others, but that he could teach by example, showing the way to understanding through his own actions.

Inspired, Naga began to emerge from the shadows, showing himself to the villagers not as a predator, but as a guardian. He watched over the crops, warding off rodents and other vermin. Gradually, the villagers began to see Naga in a different light. Fear gave way to gratitude, and in time, affection.

Years passed, and the story of the scary snake was transformed. It became that of a wise being who protected the village, a being who had learned and taught the most precious lesson of all: that of overcoming prejudice to discover the truth.

Naga was no longer alone, and the hermitage had become a meeting place where villagers brought offerings and children came to listen to the stories of the sage and the serpent, living in harmony. In the union of these two souls, one human and the other serpentine, lay the revelation of a profound Hindu truth: beyond appearances and fears, there is the essence of life, pure and unalterable, shared by all beings.

Wisdom beyond appearances

The fable of Naga the snake reminds us of the crucial importance of mutual understanding beyond prejudice. It emphasizes that fear, often born of ignorance, can be dispelled through knowledge and acceptance. Wisdom is not the prerogative of one form or species, but the quality of an open mind and generous heart. The encounter between Naga and the wise man illustrates the possibility of transcending the old stories that fuel mistrust and loneliness.

The transformation of the snake from a feared figure into a valued protector embodies the possibility of change through patience and personal example. Naga did not seek to force change among the villagers, but rather chose to live his truth, thus becoming a silent teacher of virtue. History teaches us that actions often speak louder than words, and that attitude change comes with time and observation.

Ultimately, the union between Naga and the villagers reveals that peaceful coexistence is possible when the barriers of fear are broken down. It's a reminder that behind the frightening facades we ascribe to others, there may be benevolent souls who share our desire for harmony. The true essence of life, purity of mind and heart, remains steadfast in the face of adversity, united in diversity.

7. THE BANYAN AND ITS SHADOWS

The interconnection of all living things

In the heart of the Indian forest, where the ground was woven with roots and the canopy danced with the stars, stood a majestic old Banyan tree. Its branches stretched out like welcoming arms, and its aerial roots plunged towards the earth, seeking to embrace the world. The villagers revered the tree as a silent sage, a guardian of ancient truths.

Every forest creature, from the smallest insect to the largest tiger, found refuge in its refreshing shadows. And this is where our story begins, with the Banyan whispering to the wind and sharing a secret with those who knew how to listen.

One day, as the sun painted the sky with the colors of dawn, a young monk came to meditate under the Banyan tree. His name was Bodhi, and he was seeking to understand the bond that unites all creatures in the universe. As he meditated, he heard the gentle murmur of the Banyan.

"Look beyond my roots and branches, young monk," the tree whispered. "See how I support life around me, offering shelter and nourishment, sharing water and air with the earth, connecting sky and soil."

Bodhi then observed how birds built their nests in the Banyan's crevices, how roots supported the plants around them and how fallen leaves nourished the soil, part of an endless cycle. Day turned to night, and night to day, as Bodhi stood by, listening and learning from the Banyan.

Weeks passed, and with each passing day, Bodhi saw new links, new connections. He saw how water from the nearby river hydrated the Banyan's roots, which in turn held the soil together and prevented erosion. How the Banyan's falling leaves decomposed and nourished the soil, allowing other plants to grow. How these plants fed herbivores, which fed carnivores, creating an interdependent chain of life.

One morning, as dawn broke, Bodhi finally understood the lesson the Banyan was trying to teach him. Every being, every element of nature was interconnected in a delicate and complex web. The life of one affected the life of another, and no existence was isolated. The Banyan itself was like the world in miniature, a microcosm of the entire universe.

Bodhi shared this revelation with the villagers. Beneath the Banyan, they created a sanctuary where people could come to meditate on the interconnectedness of all life. They cared for the forest as the Banyan had cared for them, protecting and preserving the balance of nature.

And so, the old Banyan became a symbol of Hindu wisdom, a constant reminder that every action has a resonance, that every life is a thread in the fabric of existence, and that the whole universe is woven into the shadows and light of the great Banyan.

Unity in the Diversity of Life

Contemplating Bodhi under the Banyan tree reveals the fundamental truth of our interdependence. In the nurturing shade of its branches, nature teaches that every life form, every element in the ecosystem, contributes to a larger balance. The Banyan becomes a living symbol of this unity, showing that the survival of one species is intrinsically linked to that of the others, and that the degradation of one part can affect the whole.

This old Banyan, in his unchanging wisdom, shares with Bodhi and the villagers the secret of existence: life is not a collection of separate entities, but a network of interwoven threads, where every action has far-reaching consequences. It's an illustration that every gesture of care or neglect towards our environment resonates through the fabric of life, influencing chains of events beyond our immediate perception.

Ultimately, the story of the Banyan and Bodhi is one of collective responsibility and reflection. By caring for our world as the Banyan cares for the forest, we honor and preserve the sacred bonds that unite all life. It's an invitation to recognize our role in maintaining nature's harmony, and to act with the awareness that our own well-being is inextricably linked to that of the environment that sustains us.

8. The Yogi and the Bandit

Transformation through compassion

In the dusty lands of Rajasthan, where the dunes undulate like inland seas, lived a yogi named Deva. His fame as a master of peace and serenity extended far beyond the surrounding villages. But this story doesn't begin with him, but with a dreaded bandit known as Viraj.

Viraj, whose heart was as hard as the leather of his boots, led his band of brigands across the desert, robbing caravans and frightening travelers. But despite his ill-gotten wealth, Viraj felt an abysmal emptiness.

One evening, as the stars wove their brilliance across the night sky, Viraj heard of Deva, the yogi who lived in a cave and was said to possess a treasure far more precious than gold. Consumed by greed, Viraj decided to seize this treasure.

He found the yogi sitting in meditation, the twilight dancing on his peaceful face. "Give me your treasure, or you'll regret it," Viraj threatened, the blade of his sword glinting menacingly.

Deva opened his eyes, and with disconcerting calm, he stared at Viraj. "The only treasure I possess is compassion," he said. "And I offer it to you, without fighting or hatred."

Viraj burst out laughing, thinking the yogi was making fun of him. But Deva invited Viraj to sit beside him and told him about his own youth, the path of suffering and rage he had taken, and how compassion had transformed him.

Hours passed as Deva shared stories from his life, evoking the healing power of compassion. Viraj, despite his resistance, found himself absorbed by the yogi's words, touched by a feeling he hadn't felt in a long time: peace.

Deva proposed that Viraj spend a week with him, promising that at the end of that week, if he still wanted the treasure, he would give it to him. Viraj agreed, driven by a curiosity he could neither understand nor deny.

For seven days and nights, Viraj learned to meditate, to nourish his body with simple food and his soul with prayers. He discovered the calm of dawn, the serenity of dusk, and for the first time, the gentle embrace of silent night. He began to feel compassion for those he had robbed, for his fellow robbers, and surprisingly, for himself.

At the end of the week, Viraj awoke transformed. He realized that Deva's treasure was not an object, but an inner wealth that no theft could bring him. With tears of awakening, he laid his sword at Deva's feet, vowing to devote his life to spreading the compassion he had received.

The once-feared bandit became a disciple of peace, and together, Viraj and Deva roamed the villages, sharing wisdom and love. And so, Deva's compassion had not only transformed a bandit, but also kindled a flame of benevolence that would light up hearts far beyond the golden dunes of Rajasthan.

The Inner Revolution through Compassion

The encounter between Deva and Viraj reveals the transformative power of compassion. Through Viraj's story, we learn that no heart is impenetrable to acts of kindness. Deva's compassion was not a weakness but a power capable of breaking through the barriers of hostility and greed. By sharing this intangible treasure, he paved the way for radical transformation, proving that understanding and love can awaken humanity in even the most hardened souls.

This tale illustrates that true wealth lies in our inner qualities, not in material possessions. Viraj, initially seduced by the promise of tangible treasure, discovers a greater good in the serenity of the mind and abundance of the heart. This realization marks not only the end of his greed, but also the beginning of a new life path marked by peace and altruism.

Deva and Viraj's story is a call to recognize the power of compassion to create lasting peace. True metamorphosis begins within, and its light can extend far beyond our own horizon.

9. THE TIGER AND THE MONK

The quest for inner peace

In the lush forests of southern India, where intertwined trees tell age-old tales, lived a tiger known for his ruthless temperament. His name was Surya, the undisputed master of these woods, feared by all creatures. But a worry gnawed at his heart, like an insidious parasite, robbing him of all inner peace.

By the river that snaked like a silver thread through the forest, a monk named Swami Anand had established his hermitage. His reputation for wisdom and tranquility was known to the men of the neighboring villages, but ignored by the wild beasts, until the day when Surya, guided by a fierce curiosity, spotted him.

The monk sat in meditation, enveloped in the melody of the wind through the branches, his mind as still as the mountain itself. Surya, intrigued by this presence that exuded such peace in stark contrast to his own restlessness, silently approached.

"Why aren't you afraid of me?" growled Surya, her fangs gleaming in the morning sun.

Swami Anand opened his eyes and met the tiger's gaze without a quiver. "Fear is like shadow, it only exists if you give it importance," he replied with enigmatic calm. "I don't nurture fear in my heart, so it can't lodge there."

Surya, baffled by this answer, sat down beside the monk. "And how can I find this peace within you?" he asked, his rough voice betraying an unsuspected vulnerability.

"By learning to look beyond your wild instincts and finding the stillness that resides within you," the monk explained. "Would you like me to teach you?"

The tiger nodded, and so began Surya's teaching. Every day, at dawn, he joined the monk and learned to control his breath, observe his thoughts and calm the tumult of his mind. The teachings were difficult for a mind as untamed as his, but Surya's determination was unrivalled.

In time, rumors of Surya's transformation spread. Forest animals began to approach without fear, and even villagers watched the strange duo from afar.

One morning, as the sun peeked through the foliage, creating a kaleidoscope of light on the forest floor, Surya finally understood. In the silence, he found an echo of the peace the monk had promised him. His heart was no longer a prisoner of rage or aggression, but beat to the rhythm of the life flowing around him.

The tiger had discovered his inner peace, not by denying his nature, but by embracing a path of serenity that coexisted with his savagery. Animals were no longer prey or threats, but companions in the eternal cycle of life.

And when Surya's last breath rose into the twilight air, years later, it was with the quietude of a spirit that had found its rest. The monk at his side murmured a blessing for the tiger's journey, testifying to an unlikely friendship forged in the tranquillity of shared existence.

The legend of Surya, the tiger who learned inner peace, flourished in the forest and beyond, reminding us that even the wildest heart can find a path to serenity.

Inner Harmony, Key to Coexistence

The story of Surya the tiger embodies the idea that inner peace is a personal quest accessible to all, regardless of an individual's intrinsic nature. It teaches that serenity is not the prerogative of human beings or naturally calm spirits alone, but can be achieved by anyone willing to embark on the path of self-reflection and self-mastery. Surya, with his wild nature, finds peace not by changing who he is, but by understanding and accepting his own deepest truths.

This fable also illustrates that true strength lies not in domination or fear, but in the ability to look beyond our primal instincts and find balance with the world around us. The monk Anand, a figure of tranquility, acts as a mirror, reflecting Surya's potential to transcend his impulses and live in harmony with his environment.

10. The Eagle and the Mantra

The ascent to the divine

In the dizzying heights of the Himalayas, where the eternal snows seem to whisper ancestral secrets, lived a majestic eagle named Garuda. His quest for ever-higher peaks was as endless as the sky itself. But even if he dominated the heavens, a deeper aspiration animated his heart: to touch the divine.

One day, hovering above the sharp ridges, Garuda caught sight of a wise man, a Rishi, immersed in deep meditation. The radiance surrounding the hermit was so intense that it seemed to create a new light in the darkness of the abyss. Driven by an unknown force, Garuda descended and perched close to the sage.

When the Rishi opened his eyes, his gaze fell on the eagle with a gentleness that seemed to embrace all creation. "Noble Garuda, what do you seek in these icy solitudes?" he asked in a voice that vibrated with the echoes of the world.

"I desire to rise, not just above the mountains but to the heights of the divine. I feel there's more than the azure sky to conquer," Garuda replied, his voice as sharp as the wind carving the peaks.

The sage, touched by the eagle's sincerity, then revealed to him a sacred mantra, a purified sound that had the power to unite the finite with the infinite, the earthly with the celestial. "Recite this mantra with unwavering devotion, and you will experience an ascent beyond all imagination," advised the Rishi.

With ardent faith, Garuda intoned the mantra. Day after day, he repeated it, his words mingling with the breath of the wind and the whiteness of the clouds. Each syllable was a wing beating towards the beyond, each repetition a flight.

Gradually, a transformation took place. Garuda felt a space open up inside him, as if each word of the mantra were weaving a web between his soul and the cosmos. He no longer simply flew; he became flight, he became the wind itself.

Days turned into months, and months into seasons. Garuda, ever more assiduous, saw his feathers tinted with gold, his eyes reflecting the stars. His cry was no longer a cry, but a perfect harmony with the song of the world.

Then, one morning, bathed in the first rays of the sun, when the mantra had become his only breath, Garuda rose. He crossed not only the limits of the atmosphere, but also those of physical existence. He flew beyond the heavens, where the gods whisper the destinies of the world, where reality fades into eternity.

Garuda was no longer an eagle but a light, a being without borders, free in the absolute. He had reached unimaginable heights, not with his wings of flesh, but with those woven by the sacred mantra.

Down on earth, the Rishi smiled, knowing that the eagle had found its ascent to the divine, not through the strength of its wings, but through the power of an eternal sound, resonating in the soul of the universe. And in the valleys and villages, they still tell the story of Garuda, the eagle who soared to embrace the divine, guided by the sacred breath of a mantra.

Elevation through Sacred Resonance

The saga of Garuda teaches us that the real frontiers are not those that stretch before our eyes, but those that reside in our hearts and minds. Like the eagle who, despite his empire in the heavens, seeks an even higher realm, the story encourages us to look beyond our tangible achievements to achieve spiritual elevation. It's a reminder that the physical conquest of the world's summits is no match for the soul's ascent to immaterial heights.

This teaching also emphasizes that devotion and perseverance are the wings on which the spiritual quest soars. Just as Garuda repeated the sacred mantra with unshakeable faith, our discipline and faith in repeating our own mantras - be they spiritual, emotional or intellectual - can lead us to unsuspected transformation and realization.

Finally, the story of Garuda illustrates that spiritual awakening transcends matter and unites us with the entire universe. The mantra doesn't just change the one who sings it, but resonates through the interweaving of all that exists, reminding us that in the resonance of the eternal, we are all connected, all part of a cosmic harmony that awaits our own voice to be complete.

11. The Shiva Stones

Hardship as an opportunity for growth

In a remote village in the foothills of the Himalayas lived a man named Arjun, known for his devotion to Shiva. Life had strewn his path with countless hardships: a harvest ravaged by storms, a river that refused to give fish, a house often visited by misfortune. Despite this, Arjun never failed to go to the temple every day, pour water over the lingam and meditate on Shiva's divine nature.

One day, as the sun declined behind the mountains, an enigmatic figure appeared before Arjun. It was a sadhu, a wandering sage, whose eyes shone with an unearthly gleam. "Why do you honor Shiva with such fervor, when your life is a web of hardship?" asked the sadhu in a voice that seemed to echo from the deep valleys.

"Trials, noble sadhu, are the stones on which Shiva invites me to build the temple of my faith," replied Arjun, his hands clasped in a gesture of respect.

The sadhu then offered Arjun three black stones, smooth and cold to the touch. "These Shiva stones are the symbol of your trials. Keep them with you, and understanding will come."

Arjun took the stones, thanking the sadhu, who disappeared as mysteriously as he had appeared. That night, Arjun placed the stones beside his altar dedicated to Shiva and fell asleep.

In his sleep, a dream visited him. He was standing in front of a large Shiva lingam, around which the three stones were arranged. Each stone was transformed into a scene from his life in which he had faced difficulties. But each time, a hand appeared, transforming hardship into blessing: devastated fields were followed by more abundant harvests, empty nets by a river teeming with fish, and his home, once filled with sorrow, now resounded with laughter and joy.

When he awoke, Arjun looked at the stones with new eyes. The trials were not curses but lessons, gifts in disguise that Shiva had given him to strengthen his mind, enlarge his heart and deepen his faith.

He picked up the stones and took them to the temple. Before the lingam, he placed them one by one, his gratitude growing with each gesture. "Om Namah Shivaya", he murmured, the words of praise rising like an offering.

Years passed, and the village prospered. The Shiva stones, once symbols of hardship, were now integrated into the temple wall, reminding everyone that life's difficulties can become cornerstones of wisdom and strength.

Arjun, aging but quick-witted, often told the village children the story of the Shiva stones, teaching that every trial is an opportunity offered by the divine to grow, elevate and draw closer to the source of all existence.

And in the whisper of the wind, some could hear the voice of Shiva, whispering through time and space, reminding us that every moment of challenge is a step closer to the eternal dance of life.

The Wisdom of Trials

In the story of Arjun and the Shiva Stones, we discover that trials are not obstacles, but milestones on the path to enlightenment. Arjun's difficulties are not punishments, but invitations to resilience and faith. It teaches us that the attitude with which we face adversity can transform our destiny. Trials can be blessers in disguise, silent teachers who shape our endurance and wisdom.

The black stones, symbols of Arjun's challenges, become cornerstones of his spiritual growth. This symbolizes that our perception of hardship can change dramatically when we recognize its potential to help us build a stronger edifice of character. Difficulties are not ends in themselves, but passages leading us to a deeper understanding of life.

Finally, the legend of Arjun reminds us that gratitude is a transformative force. By welcoming every challenge with gratitude, we invite unsuspected abundance into our lives.

12. The Dance of Parvati

Striking a balance

In an ancient village nestled in the heart of India lived a dancer named Anika, famous for her breathtaking performances of traditional Bharatanatyam dance. She had devoted her life to perfecting her art, to the point where dancing was not just a part of her life, but her whole life. However, despite her dedication and impeccable technique, Anika felt that something essential was missing: the balance between the rigor of discipline and the spontaneous joy of freedom.

Every evening, after her performances, Anika would go to an old temple dedicated to the goddess Parvati, hoping to find the key to what she was missing. She prayed fervently, asking the goddess to help her unite the structure of her dance with the free expression of her soul.

One full-moon night, while Anika was absorbed in her prayer, she was enveloped in a soft, warm light. The goddess Parvati materialized before her in an aura of divine grace. Anika bowed deeply, moved by this apparition.

Parvati, with a smile as tender as the evening breeze, spoke to her: "Anika, your dedication to dance has touched me. However, you must learn that true mastery of the art lies in the balance between precision and letting go. Let me show you."

The goddess began to dance. Her movements embodied technical perfection, each step and gesture the very essence of the discipline. But as she danced, her dance evolved and became imbued with spontaneity and freedom. Each free movement seemed to spring naturally from the structure that preceded it, as if discipline and freedom were not two distinct concepts, but rather two halves of a harmonious whole.

Anika watched, wide-eyed, as the goddess's lesson permeated her heart and mind. She understood that discipline was the foundation that would allow her to explore the infinite reaches of creative freedom. The structure of dance was not a chain, but the wings that would allow her to fly.

At dawn, the goddess disappeared as subtly as she had appeared, leaving Anika alone with the revelation that had lit up her soul. That day, and all the days that followed, Anika danced like she'd never danced before. Her dancing was still precise and disciplined, but now she infused it with a joy and spontaneity that delighted her audience in a whole new way.

Anika became a legend, not only for her technical mastery but for the vitality and passion that emanated from each performance. She was living proof that by balancing discipline and freedom, one could reach the heights of artistic expression.

Parvati's dance had become her own, a dance where every step, however measured, was a heartbeat towards infinity. And in every corner of India where her steps echoed, the echo of the balance struck between discipline and freedom inspired the hearts and minds of all who watched her.

Harmony between Discipline and Freedom

Anika's quest and her encounter with the goddess Parvati teach the importance of balance in the pursuit of excellence. Her experience illustrates that mastery is found not only in the rigor of practice, but also in embracing spontaneity. This resonates with the universal truth that in every area of life, a balance between structure and fluidity is essential to achieving full and authentic expression.

Anika's story reveals that discipline is the foundation for the elevation of the creative spirit, not a hindrance to freedom. The structure of discipline creates a framework in which freedom can flourish, suggesting that these two elements are not contradictory but complementary. Their harmonious alliance leads to a form of expression that transcends the boundaries of technique and touches the heart of art.

Finally, Anika's incarnation as a complete artist is a reminder that the balance achieved in any practice can inspire and influence far beyond the individual. Her transformation not only delights her audience but also sows seeds of inspiration, showing that the union of discipline and freedom is a powerful force that can elevate not only the artist, but art itself.

13. The Chariot and Karma

The wheels of destiny

In a small village on the banks of the sacred Ganges River, there lived a cartwright named Arjun, who built carts. Arjun was known for his exceptional talent, but also for his tendency to bend the rules of business ethics. He wasn't above substituting inferior lumber on occasion to boost his profits. He didn't consider the consequences, concentrating solely on immediate gain.

One day, a wise man came to the village. Observing Arjun's work, he ordered a cart, specifying that it had to be ready for the festival of Dussehra, to transport the idol of Lord Rama to the temple. Arjun saw an opportunity for a bargain and agreed, promising that the cart would be the sturdiest and most majestic the village had ever seen.

The sage, having heard of Arjun's dubious practices, said to him in a quiet voice: "Don't forget, Arjun, that every wheel you build turns not only around its own axis, but also within the great cycle of karma." Arjun laughed softly at the warning and continued his work, ignoring the sage's words.

When the party arrived, the carriage was ready. It was splendid to look at, but Arjun had been true to form and used inferior wood for the wheels, hiding its flaws under a glossy varnish. The wise man took his place in the cart, and the procession began.

At first, all went according to plan, but as they passed through the village, a wheel broke, causing the idol to fall. A shockwave swept through the crowd. The idol was unharmed, but the incident was seen as a very bad omen. The villagers' anger turned to Arjun, who could only bow his head in shame.

The sage climbed down from the cart and walked towards Arjun, who was expecting harsh words. But, with compassion, the sage said: "Arjun, the cartwheel you built was destined to collapse, because it wasn't made with integrity. In the same way, our actions, good or bad, come back to us, just as the wheels of a chariot return to the same point after completing their cycle."

It was a revelation for Arjun. He understood that, like the wheels of a wagon, every action he took left an imprint on the path of his destiny. Arjun asked the sage and the villagers for forgiveness, pledging to repair not only the wagon but also his professional ethics.

In time, Arjun became a renowned cartwright, known for his integrity and the quality of his carts. He often taught village children that just as sturdy wheels carry a cart safely to its destination, good deeds sustain a life and lead to a propitious destiny.

And every Dussehra, as the procession passed by, Arjun's sturdy, reliable chariot carried the idol of Lord Rama without incident, a living illustration of karma, the eternal law of the just return of things.

Integrity and the Wheel of Destiny

The story of Arjun, the cart driver, underlines the fundamental value of integrity in life and business. When Arjun chooses profit over quality, he learns a vital lesson about how our actions determine our future. This teaching reflects the principle of karma, which asserts that every action has a consequence, an echo in the fabric of the universe that will return to its point of origin with infallible precision.

The fall of Arjun's chariot idol is not just an unfortunate incident, but a powerful symbol of the reality that compromising on our principles can lead to ruin, even if the intention was to achieve immediate success. This part of the story reveals that actions motivated by greed or deceit are ultimately counter-productive and will lead to the loss of trust and honor, two invaluable assets in all spheres of life.

Arjun's turnaround after his realization embodies hope and redemption. It teaches that, whatever our past mistakes, it's always possible to right the course and align ourselves with the principles of honesty and responsibility.

14. Rama and the Old Bridge

Faith as a foundation

In the kingdom of Kosala, Prince Rama was faced with a monumental challenge. His beloved Sita had been kidnapped by the demon Ravana and taken across the ocean to the kingdom of Lanka. To save her, Rama had to build a bridge across the stormy sea, but despite his courage and strength, the task seemed impossible.

Rama and his faithful brother Lakshmana were standing on the shore, watching the furious waves, when they were joined by their army of valiant and devoted monkeys, led by Hanuman, the most loyal of them all. The monkeys were ready to do anything to help Rama, but even their combined strength didn't seem enough to build a bridge over such an impetuous sea.

It was then that Rama turned to the ocean and began to pray. He prayed for a sign, for divine help, for he knew that only an act of faith could lead them to victory. His prayers were answered, and the ocean itself calmed, the waves subsiding as if by magic, revealing a chain of submerged rocks.

The monkeys set to work, carrying stones and rocks to build the bridge. But every stone they laid fell into the abyss, swallowed up by the waters. It was then that Rama had a vision of Vishwakarma, the divine architect, who whispered in his ear that everyone's faith was the key.

Rama turned to Hanuman and said, "Write my name on the stones, for it is faith that will keep them afloat." Hanuman, though perplexed, did as he was told. The moment Rama's name was inscribed on the stones, they miraculously floated on the water. The bridge took shape, supported not by the stone, but by pure faith in Rama's virtue.

Day and night, the work continued, the stones engraved with Rama's name linking together, creating a passageway across the sea. The monkey army was soon joined by the inhabitants of neighboring villages, touched by Rama's devotion and courage. Every stone laid was a prayer, and the bridge a monument to the power of faith.

Finally, the bridge was completed and Rama, with his army, crossed over to Lanka. A great battle ensued, but with the help of faith and his devoted allies, Rama defeated Ravana and saved Sita.

The old bridge, built on faith, stood for centuries, a silent testimony to what unshakeable faith in what is right and pure can achieve. Later generations were reminded that when faced with the insurmountable, it is faith that provides the foundation for overcoming obstacles and uniting people in a common purpose.

Thus, the story of Rama and the old bridge reminds us that the strongest foundations, those that can carry a man through the most violent storms, are not made of stone or wood, but of unshakeable faith in virtue and righteousness.

Faith and Perseverance in Adversity

The story of Rama and the old bridge embodies the power of faith in the face of seemingly insurmountable obstacles. It teaches us that faith in virtue and in the rightness of our path can initiate miracles and provide the unexpected support needed to overcome challenges. This story reminds us that faith is more than a belief; it's an active force that, when truly embraced, has the power to change the tangible world around us.

Building the bridge was not just a work of engineering, but also a demonstration of collective confidence. It demonstrates how shared faith and concerted action can create the impossible, a bridge between hope and realization. It inspires us to work together with a common purpose, reinforcing the idea that collective faith in a cause can lift mountains and build bridges over life's stormy seas.

Finally, the legend of the Bridge of Rama provides a metaphor for our own journey. It suggests that when we carve our deepest convictions into the foundations of our actions, we can keep our dreams afloat, even in the depths of adversity. Perseverance guided by unshakeable faith is the cornerstone that sustains great designs, and it is this that leads us to victory over our own inner demons and storms.

15. The Monkey and the Illusion

Reality beyond perception

In the depths of a lush forest, where the sun filters through the dense foliage, lived a mischievous monkey named Kapil. Renowned for his mischief, Kapil loved to fool his jungle friends with tricks and illusions. His latest trick was to reflect light through crystals to create fake waterfalls on barren trees, much to the amazement of thirsty animals.

One day, while exploring a remote part of the forest, Kapil found an old mirror, abandoned by a stranger. Fascinated by his own reflection, he thought he was playing with another monkey. Day after day, he brought his "new friend" fruit, told stories and shared his secrets, without ever receiving an answer. Kapil's loneliness finally seemed to ease in the presence of this silent companion.

However, Kapil's life was turned upside down by an unexpected incident. As a violent storm broke out, lightning struck a tree, which collapsed on the mirror, shattering it into a thousand pieces. Kapil was horrified to see his friend "disappear". In a fit of despair, he reached into the debris and found a piece of weathered paper. It was a letter written by a traveler who, years before, had been lost and alone in this very forest. The letter spoke of self-discovery and the importance of the company of others.

Kapil, reading the traveler's trembling words, realized the lesson the mirror had taught him: the reality of his existence lay not in this mute reflection, but in the living, responsive relationships he shared with his jungle friends. The monkey, known to all for his illusions, had himself been the victim of an illusion, seeking companionship in lifeless reflections.

With this realization, Kapil returned to his friends. He worked hard to gain their trust, now using his ingenuity to help them rather than deceive them. He revealed where to find real water sources, shared food without deceit, and his stories were no longer tissue of lies, but enriching accounts of his adventures and mistakes.

In time, the forest resounded with laughter and song, not because of Kapil's tricks, but because of his new authenticity. Animals, once cautious and wary, now gathered around him to hear his true stories and share the warmth of true friendship.

Reality, Kapil had learned, lay not in the illusions he created, but in the bonds he forged with sincerity. The monkey who had loved illusions had finally discovered the sweetest of truths: that reality, with its imperfections and surprises, was far more beautiful and gratifying than any mirage.

Truth at the Heart of Relationships

The story of Kapil the monkey illustrates the importance of sincerity and authenticity in building genuine relationships. Believing he had found companionship in a lifeless reflection, Kapil misunderstood the nature of connection and friendship. Illusion may offer temporary comfort, but it can never replace the warmth and reciprocity of a genuine exchange with another. This teaches us that authentic presence is the foundation on which deep and lasting bonds are built.

The shattering of the mirror symbolizes a moment of revelation, a pivot where illusion gives way to reality. Kapil, confronted with the truth of his loneliness, realizes that relationships based on deception or illusion are as fragile as glass. He understands that only relationships forged in truth can survive the storms of life. It's a lesson for us all: value and cultivate transparency with those around us.

Finally, Kapil shows us that personal transformation is possible when we acknowledge our mistakes and learn from them. The story encourages us to let go of false self-images and embrace our authenticity. In the acceptance of our reality, with all its imperfections, lies the beauty of authentic human connection. It is in this space of truth that we find the most lasting joy and satisfaction.

16. The Antelope and Meditation

Perseverance towards awakening

In a peaceful clearing lined with frangipani trees and lotus floating on tranquil waters, lived an antelope named Asha. She was unrivalled in her agility, but lived in constant fear of being hunted by predators. One day, fleeing from a tiger, Asha ventured into an unknown part of the forest and came upon an old ruined temple, where the statue of a meditating sage seemed to radiate a calming presence.

Exhausted and hopeless, Asha collapsed in front of the statue and fell asleep. When she awoke, she watched in wonder as the flowers around her seemed more alive, and the air was vibrant with serene energy. An ancient, gentle voice came to her, saying that true peace lay not in escape, but in deep understanding of oneself and the world.

Asha, intrigued and desperate to find a solution to her precarious situation, decided to take the advice to heart. She began to meditate, seeking to soak up the tranquility of the place. Day after day, she sat silently, learning to quiet her mind and look within herself. She meditated on the rhythm of nature, the growth of trees and the cycle of the seasons.

Over time, her perception changed. She felt unity with the forest and even with its predators. She saw that they were not her enemies, but living beings in their own right. Her fear was slowly transformed into understanding, then compassion. Asha was no longer guided by fear, but by a new clarity.

As she reached this heightened state of consciousness, predators began to perceive her differently. They no longer saw her as prey, but as a creature possessing an aura of wisdom and peace, which they dared not disturb. They would approach her, sniff her curiously, then leave, as if touched by the tranquility emanating from her.

One day, an old tiger approached her and sat down beside her, sharing this moment of silence. It was the same tiger that had chased her in her past life of fear and flight. In the shared silence, a mutual understanding grew between the antelope and the tiger, transcending the laws of nature.

Asha became a symbol of peace for all beings in the forest, and the old ruined temple a gathering place for those seeking harmony. Animals, once in competition with each other, now gathered in the clearing, bathed in the peaceful energy Asha had cultivated.

By seeking peace to escape her fears, Asha not only found her own enlightenment but also transformed her environment. Meditation had given her an inner sanctuary from which sprang an outer haven, where predation gave way to peaceful coexistence. His story taught that even in the midst of the most instinctive fear, it's possible to find the light of consciousness that unifies and protects.

Transcendent Awakening

Asha the antelope teaches us that inner peace transforms our perception of the outside world. Her quest for serenity through meditation reveals that understanding and accepting one's deepest nature can transcend the instincts of fear and survival. It shows that peace is not a destination but a path, a moment-by-moment practice that requires perseverance and courage. Inner tranquillity is a powerful catalyst for change, capable of influencing our environment and the beings around us.

Asha's change of perspective, from prey to peace, shows that our state of mind can influence our relationships with others. Fear and competition give way to mutual understanding when we rise above our primal instincts. Predators recognizing the aura of wisdom and peace around Asha illustrate how tranquility can engender mutual respect, transcending roles predetermined by nature.

17. Saraswati's Mirror

The power of knowledge

In a small village where the rivers whispered ancient tales and the breezes carried the aroma of jasmine, there lived a young boy named Veer. Veer was curious and eager to learn, but in his village, books were rare and storytellers even rarer. He spent his days dreaming of worlds hidden behind the veils of knowledge, worlds he could never reach.

One full-moon night, when the stars seemed to whisper to each other, Veer ventured out of bed and walked to the old banyan tree, his heart heavy with an insatiable desire for knowledge. Under the tree, a soft, silvery light danced across the grass, and Veer saw something he'd never seen before: a beautifully chiselled mirror, seemingly floating unsupported.

In the mirror's reflection, he saw a woman of serene beauty, draped in a white sari adorned with gold and carrying a vînâ, an Indian instrument. It was Saraswati, the goddess of knowledge. She gave him a benevolent smile and spoke to him in a voice as clear and melodious as the course of a river.

"Veer, you have sought knowledge with perseverance, but knowledge is not only in books or in the words of the wise. It's in every stone, every leaf and every breath of wind. But to see it, you must desire it with sincerity and seek it with pure intention."

Then she placed her hand on the mirror, and the glass began to ripple like water. Through this moving surface, Veer saw not his own reflection, but scenes of great learning and discovery. He saw mathematicians tracing geometrical figures, philosophers debating under trees, stars named by astronomers and healers gathering rare herbs.

"What you see are fragments of knowledge scattered across the world and time," says Saraswati, "It's in every quest, every question, every exploration. Knowledge is the mirror through which the soul understands itself and the universe."

The mirror became crystal clear, and Veer saw his own reflection. But in his eyes was a new spark of understanding and revelation. The boy knew then that he didn't need books to begin his journey: every experience was a page, every observation a chapter.

When Veer turned around, the goddess had disappeared, but the mirror was still there. He took it back to the village, where it became the starting point of his apprenticeship. Every reflection became a lesson, every image a discovery.

In time, Veer became a sage himself, teaching others what the goddess of knowledge had revealed to him. Saraswati's mirror had shown a child that the thirst for knowledge was the greatest power, that every curiosity could be a guide, and that knowledge was a never-ending quest.

And so, the story of Veer and Saraswati's mirror spanned the ages, teaching that the power of knowledge resides in everyone, waiting to be reflected in the actions and thoughts of those who seek with heart.

The Eternal Quest for Knowledge

The legend of Veer and the mirror of Saraswati reveal that knowledge is a timeless journey that extends far beyond written pages and spoken words. It is omnipresent, woven into the fabric of the universe, accessible to those who seek with passion and sincerity. This story teaches us that every element of nature is a silent teacher, every experience a valuable lesson, and curiosity is the key that opens all doors of perception.

Veer's dialogue with the goddess Saraswati underlines that the thirst for knowledge is the most powerful power that resides within us. It illuminates the understanding that knowledge is not a possession to be acquired, but a presence to be recognized and explored. The mirror symbolizes the inner reflection through which the soul learns to read the great book of existence, of which every moment is a page laden with meaning.

By becoming a teacher himself, Veer embodies the ultimate truth that knowledge grows through sharing. His transformation from solitary dreamer to community sage demonstrates that learning is both personal and universal.

18. Brahma's Bird

The song of the soul

In the deep, ancient forests of Bharat, where the secrets of the world are whispered by the wind through the leaves, there lived a bird with azure feathers and a melodious song, but who didn't yet know the reach of his own voice. This little bird, named Neela, was content to hum simple melodies, unaware of the unsuspected power of her own song.

One morning, as dawn stretched its rosy fingers across the sky, Neela rose above the canopy to welcome the sun. As she sang, the world seemed to stop and listen, but Neela was oblivious to the magic awakening unbeknownst to her.

It was then that Brahma, the Creator, fell in love with Neela's sincerity and decided to visit her in the guise of an old sage. He appeared on Neela's favorite branch as she finished her morning melody.

"Neela," he said with a smile in his voice, "you sing every day, but do you know the true power of your singing?"

Neela, intrigued but not frightened, gently shook her head, her feathers gleaming under the first rays of the sun.

Brahma, with fatherly tenderness, then revealed: "In your song lies the ability to touch souls, heal hearts, and inspire hope. Your song is a precious gift, a hymn that can unite all creatures in a moment of pure harmony."

Neela, though humble, found it hard to believe these words. How could a simple bird have such an impact?

To show her, Brahma placed a delicate feather on the bird's heart and sang a pure note. The note penetrated Neela, who felt a new strength flowing through her veins. Driven by divine inspiration, Neela took flight and, instinctively, her song soared above the trees, clearer, more powerful and imbued with a celestial sweetness.

As Neela sang, the forest animals came to a halt. The wind calmed, the rivers slowed their course, and even the trees seemed to lean closer to listen. Her hymn traveled through valleys and over mountains, touching the heart of every living creature.

The tigers ceased their hunt, the deer forgot their fear, and the birds joined Neela in a chorus that reached to the heavens. For the first time in eons, absolute peace reigned in the forest, and all living beings shared a moment of perfect unity.

When the chanting ended, Neela, exhausted but exhilarated, returned to her branch. She saw the old sage transform into divine light, and realized that she had been blessed by Brahma himself.

From then on, Neela sang every day, no longer out of habit, but with an awareness of the gift she had been given. Her hymn became a daily reminder that every creature, big or small, possesses within it a unique song - a song of the soul that can bring harmony to the world. And in the heart of every being who heard her song, a glimmer of hope was born, a desire to live in peace with all the other inhabitants of the forest.

The story of Neela and her divine hymn became part of the legends of Bharat, teaching generations that the song of the soul can transcend differences and unite the world in a symphony of love and peace.

The Inner Hymn of Connection

The fable of Neela, the bird blessed by Brahma, teaches us the inestimable value of recognizing and sharing our innate gifts. It suggests that every individual, no matter how seemingly simple or modest in stature, carries within him or her an immense potential which, when revealed and expressed, has the power to transform not only the bearer of the gift but also the world around him or her.

This legend illustrates that the sincere expression of our essence can have a profound and healing impact on those around us. Neela's song was not just a string of melodious notes, it was a unifying force that reminds us that beauty and purity of intention are capable of transcending divisions and engendering harmony. It's a call to search within ourselves for that unique melody that can bring peace and unity.

The bird's song is a metaphor for our own power to inspire positive change and create ripples of impact far beyond our immediate environment. We are all called to find our own "soul song" to participate in the great symphony of life.

19. The Deer and the Mandala

The journey to the center

In the serene valley of Siddhartha, bordered by gentle hills and singing rivers, lived an eloquent deer named Darshana. His tawny coat shimmered in the sunlight as if he were the guardian of autumn colors. Darshana was known for his unwavering curiosity, but also for his deep desire to understand his place in the universe.

One day, as dawn painted the sky in shades of purple and gold, Darshana came across a giant mandala, traced on the forest floor with divine precision. Powders of every color formed hypnotic patterns, inviting the viewer on an introspective journey. Without understanding why, Darshana was called to the center of this ephemeral work of art.

With trembling hesitation, he placed one hoof after another on the mandala, and as soon as he was inside, the outside world seemed to fade away. Each step led him through circles of patterns that told stories of stars and moons, mountains and rivers, birth, life, death and rebirth.

The colors danced and vibrated, guiding Darshana deeper into the mandala. He saw light and shadow playing on the canvas of reality, scenes of wild and peaceful life following one another as if in a trance. Each circle he crossed seemed to dissipate a layer of his being, revealing truths he had long sought.

After what seemed an instant and an eternity, Darshana reached the center of the mandala. There, in a circle of pure light, he saw a golden deer, his double, staring back at him with eyes filled with infinite wisdom.

"Who are you?" asked Darshana, her voice trembling with wonder.

"I am you," replied the golden stag. "I am who you really are, beyond fears, doubts and illusions. I am your strength and wisdom, your courage and peace. You have passed through the layers of existence to find me here, at the center of your being."

Darshana then understood that the journey through the mandala was not just an outer journey, but an inner one. The golden stag was the manifestation of her true self, the essence that remained when all else was stripped away.

With a new understanding, Darshana was suddenly taken back to the beginning of the mandala, each color, each line gently fading behind him. He returned to the forest, but he was no longer the same deer. He now carried within him the calm of the mandala's center, a serenity that would never leave him.

From that day on, Darshana lived with a harmony that even the leaves dancing in the wind seemed to recognize. He shared his experience with others, not with words, but with the peace he radiated.

As for the mandala, it was carried away by the valley wind, as if to remind us that the quest for self is as impermanent and changeable as the seasons. But the journey Darshana had undertaken was eternal, engraved in her soul like the stars in the night sky.

At the Centre of Self

Darshana's quest through the mandala is a powerful metaphor for introspection, inviting us to recognize that the path to wisdom and inner peace is as complex and colorful as the mandala itself. It reminds us that to find our true essence, we must have the courage to explore the deepest layers of our consciousness, accepting that this journey may challenge our most ingrained perceptions.

This story illustrates the transformation that takes place when we confront our own inner reflection. Like Darshana, we're all searching for answers, and often it's by venturing into the depths of our being that we encounter our "golden stag", our truest and wisest self. This inner journey is a necessary passage for those who aspire to wholeness and serenity.

Finally, history teaches us that the peace found at the center of our personal mandala is a treasure to be cherished, but it is as ephemeral as art in sand. It's essential to share this peace not through words, but through the harmony of our existence.

20. The Vishnu Ladder

The ladder of spirituality

In the ancient village of Dharapur, where the rivers whispered prayers and the wind carried legends, there lived a simple man named Veer. His days were devoted to his work in the rice fields and his nights to the stars, seeking to understand the mysteries of existence.

One night, under the benevolent light of the full moon, Veer had a dream in which the god Vishnu appeared to him, bursting with a bluish aura. "Veer," said Vishnu with a voice that seemed to weave space around them, "you seek the rungs of spirituality, and I have come to offer you a path."

Before Veer stood a golden ladder, ascending to the heavens, each rung glittering with a different light. Vishnu continued, "Each rung represents a stage of awakening. Climb up and learn."

When he awoke, Veer found, to his amazement, the ladder he'd dreamed of leaning against his house. Amazed, he placed his foot on the first step and felt a gentle warmth flow through him. "Ahimsa", non-violence, whispered the wind. He rose with compassion, freeing his heart of all bitterness.

The second step shone with an introspective light. "Satya", the truth. Memories of half-truths and white lies came to mind. Veer accepted them, then released them with a sigh, feeling more authentic and pure.

The third step pulsated with the vigor of life. "Asteya", the non-theft. He thought of the times when he had envied the harvests of others, when his gaze had desired more than his share. On this step, he learned to appreciate sufficiency, to cherish the abundance of his own harvest.

Each step taught him a new virtue, from "Brahmacharya", moderation, to "Aparigraha", non-attachment. Greed, anger and delusion were all washed away as he climbed towards the stars.

The last rungs were the most testing. "Dharana", concentration, forced him to focus his mind, shutting out all distractions. Then came "Dhyana", deep meditation, where Veer plunged into an inner silence so profound that even the beat of his heart seemed like a distant drum.

At last, Veer reached the final rung. "Samadhi", oneness with the universe. It stretched out above him like a portal, vibrating with a celestial symphony. With a mixture of fear and wonder, Veer clung to it and was absorbed in a swirl of stars.

When Veer came to, dawn caressed the horizon with its colorful palette. The ladder had disappeared, but the transformation in him was tangible. Every action, every word, every thought was imbued with the wisdom of the rungs he had climbed.

Veer was no longer just a man from the village, he was a living example of spirituality incarnate. And although Vishnu's ladder was no longer visible, Veer's ascent to enlightenment remained etched in the echo of his footsteps, in the smile he offered the world and in the peace that inhabited him, as unshakeable as the earth beneath his feet.

Steps to Awakening

Veer's story reminds us that the quest for spirituality is not an external undertaking but an inner journey, where each step, each awareness, each surge of virtue is a rung on the ladder of our own evolution. This ascent is not measured by the distance covered, but by the transformation that each virtue, each awareness brings to our soul. Like Veer, we can find in the universal principles of truth, non-violence and non-attachment the foundations for a life imbued with spirituality.

The vision of Vishnu's ladder also suggests that spiritual awakening is within the reach of all those who aspire to rise above the triviality of material existence. Each rung of the ladder represents a personal and spiritual challenge to be overcome, and it is in the effort to overcome these challenges that genuine and lasting growth is found.

Finally, the ladder that disappeared at dawn signifies that, although teachings may be ephemeral, their imprint is indelible in the essence of those who have experienced them. Veer's awakening underlines that the lessons of spirituality transcend their mystical origins to become rooted in everyday life, resonating in the peace and harmony that naturally emanate from those who have touched the unity of existence.

21. The Butterfly and the Vedas

The metamorphosis of knowledge

In the tranquil valley of Vidya, where every stone and leaf seemed to be reciting Vedic hymns, a yellow butterfly twirled, splashing the air with its vibrant wings. His name was Vyan, and unlike his peers, he wasn't content with flower nectar. Vyan sought to imbibe a deeper knowledge, that inscribed in the Vedas, the sacred texts of ancient wisdom.

One day, as Vyan explored the heart of the valley, he found a secret cave, where rishis of the past had engraved sacred hymns on the walls. As he fluttered among the sacred verses, he felt a strange energy envelop him.

Every wingbeat sounded a mantra, and every mantra pulsed through his fragile being. It was as if the echoes of distant sages were singing through him. Days passed, and Vyan, hypnotized by the chanting of the Vedas, learned them by heart, letting the vibrations metamorphose him, not physically, but spiritually.

This ancient wisdom was his only source of nourishment. The mantras of the Rigveda taught him the harmony of the cosmos. The Yajurveda revealed to him the meaning of sacrifice and action. The songs of the Samaveda taught him to listen to the symphony of creation, and the Atharvaveda offered him the secrets of healing and protection.

In time, the color of his wings became the azure of the heavens, the gold of the dawns and the ebony of moonless nights. The people of the valley began to talk about the butterfly with the wings of truth, the one who reflected the wisdom of the ages. They came to the cave to catch a glimpse of Vyan, hoping to capture a fragment of truth in her beauty.

But Vyan's transformation was far more profound. He wasn't just changing himself; he was changing those around him. When he danced in the air, children stopped to contemplate, intuitively touched by peace. Adults, exhausted by the cares of daily life, found comfort and inspiration in the tranquility he embodied.

Finally, after months of communion with the Vedas, Vyan realized that his metamorphosis was approaching its apogee. He landed in the center of the cave and wrapped himself in a cocoon of pure energy, chanting the mantras he had internalized.

When he emerged, he was no longer a butterfly. He had become a light, a Vedic spark incarnate, devoid of form but rich in essence. He soared, melting into the winds, and with him, knowledge.

It is said that since that day, when a seeker wanders off into meditation, he can sometimes hear the brushing of wings and feel the caress of knowledge. For Vyan, the butterfly and the Vedas, had taught the valley that knowledge is not just to be read or heard, but to be lived and transformed into wisdom.

And so, Vyan's metamorphosis was not the end, but the beginning of an eternal transmission of knowledge, resonating throughout the valley of Vidya, touching every soul ready to listen, ready to be transformed.

The Dance of Eternal Knowledge

The odyssey of Vyan, the knowledge-hungry butterfly, teaches us that the quest for knowledge transcends the physical form. Like Vyan, we are all invited not simply to consume information, but to let it penetrate and transform us from within. True wisdom is not a goal, but a path, a continuous metamorphosis that leads us to reflect the light of eternal truths through the colorful wings of our existence.

Vyan's journey into the cave of Vedic mantras emphasizes that knowledge is not confined to written words or speeches, but is a vibrant experience, a song that resonates within us and awakens us to a higher consciousness. Learning then becomes a sacred act, a dance with the universe where every movement, every pulse is a step closer to our spiritual fulfillment.

Vyan's ascension to the state of light perpetuates the idea that we too can become vectors of wisdom, silently but profoundly influencing the world around us, long after our visible presence has ceased to be.

22. Ganesha and the Honey Pot

Obstacles as teachers

In a forest where the trees whispered ancient legends, there lived a young bear named Daloo, his coat as black as the moonless night. Daloo's life was simple and peaceful, punctuated by the seasons and his quest for honey, his favorite delicacy.

One day, while searching for his precious food, Daloo found a honeypot sitting at the base of a tree. It was strangely smooth and shiny, as if fashioned by the gods themselves. Daloo, with his insatiable appetite, tried to reach the honey, but with each attempt, the pot slipped away, sliding between his paws with surprising agility.

Daloo's frustration grew with each failure, but he was determined. He tried day and night, using every trick and every ounce of strength he possessed. But the jar remained unattainable, as if it contained not honey, but a well-kept secret.

It was then that Ganesha, the elephant-headed god, appeared before Daloo. The deity was known for placing and removing obstacles on the path of life. Daloo, knowing the legends, bowed respectfully to the god.

"Ganesha, O divine sage, why can't I reach that honey?" he asked, his heart heavy.

Ganesha, with a mischievous smile, replied: "Daloo, this obstacle is not here to torment you, but to teach you. Look beyond your quest for honey, and you'll see a deeper truth."

Daloo, perplexed, looked at the pot, but this time with fresh eyes. He saw that every time he stretched out his paw, his reflection in the shiny jar showed him a different aspect of himself: his impatience, his frustration, his relentlessness. The honeypot was like a mirror to his soul.

Inspired by this revelation, Daloo took a deep breath and decided to simply sit, observe and meditate on his actions and desires. The days passed, and with them, his thirst for honey turned into a thirst for knowledge. The obstacle had forced him to look inward, develop patience and appreciate the honey of wisdom more than that of greed.

When Ganesha returned, he saw a changed Daloo, calmer and wiser. "You've learned your lesson, Daloo," Ganesha said approvingly. "The obstacle of the honeypot has opened the way to greater understanding for you. So, it's time for the obstacle to disappear."

With a flick of his trunk, Ganesha steadied the pot and Daloo was finally able to taste the honey. But the bear didn't pounce on it greedily. He gratefully took a small amount, savoring the sweetness that was more than just a taste, for it was tinged with the sweetness of acquired wisdom.

Thus, Ganesha taught Daloo and those who heard of the story that life's obstacles, however frustrating, can become our greatest teachers, revealing hidden truths and leading to growth that even the sweetest honey could not match.

The Honey Pot Reflection

The tale of Daloo and the Elusive Pot reveals profound wisdom about the nature of obstacles. They are not mere hindrances, but instruments of divine teaching. Ganesha, in his benevolent malice, guides the black bear not towards immediate gratification, but towards fertile introspection. History shows us that our greatest frustrations can become mirrors, reflecting the parts of our being that need attention and growth.

Daloo's determination to reach the honey illustrates our own tendency to fight challenges with strength and determination. But sometimes, it's in the pause, in the reflective calm in the face of the obstacle, that true understanding emerges. This story invites us to recognize patience and meditation as powerful tools for transforming our raw desires into gentler, deeper quests for wisdom.

When we embrace the lessons hidden behind our trials, we taste a satisfaction far more exquisite than immediate gratification - that of wisdom and personal evolution.

23. The River and the Aatman

The flow of identity

Once upon a time, a river named Saraswati flowed through the fertile land of India. It meandered gracefully through forests and plains, nurturing life wherever it went. But deep in its course, a doubt tormented her: who was she really? Was she just a stream destined to melt into the immensity of the ocean, or was there more to her?

This turmoil deepened when she heard the villagers speak of the Aatman, the eternal soul that infuses all life.

"Am I more than a river? Do I have an Aatman too?" she wondered.

Saraswati decided to meditate on her true nature. She slowed her course and plunged into a state of deep reflection, losing herself in the meanders of her thoughts as she wrapped herself around trees and rocks.

One day, a wise man crossed his path. He stopped to drink from her clear water and sensed her trouble. "Why are you so troubled, noble Saraswati?" he asked.

The river confided its doubts and fears to him, telling him about the Aatman and his desire to understand his own essence.

The sage, touched by the river's sincerity, said: "You are the water that gives life, and in this, you are a manifestation of Brahman, the ultimate reality. Your Aatman is not distinct from the Aatman that resides in every being. Like water, you are both form and formless, tangible and intangible."

The sage's words made their way through Saraswati's mind, and she began to think more deeply. She realized that, just as she took the form of the river, waterfalls, streams or even rain, her Aatman took on different forms while remaining the same eternal essence.

Saraswati then saw the diversity of life that flourished along its shores and understood that, in the same way, the Aatman manifested itself uniquely in each creature. She didn't need to merge with the ocean to find her identity; she was already a complete and perfect expression of the divine.

In this awareness, Saraswati ceased to see herself as an isolated entity. She understood that every drop of water, every stream, every valley she passed through was a dance of the Aatman, playing through her the eternal cycle of creation. And so Saraswati continued to flow, no longer with questions, but with a new understanding of her true nature. She was neither just a river, nor just part of the hydrological cycle, but a divine entity, a reflection of the Aatman who unites all things.

Saraswati realized that her question had never been whether she was more than a river, but to recognize that, in every curve and wave, the Aatman was revealing himself, teaching those who listen that we are all manifestations of the one universal consciousness.

The Essence of Existence

Saraswati's quest to understand her identity reflects our own search for meaning in an ever-changing world. Her realization that she is more than just a river reminds us that our identity is not limited to the form or function we occupy in society. We are all embodiments of a larger essence, connected to a universal source of energy and existence, Brahman. This understanding broadens our perspective of who we are and our place in the universe.

The interaction between Saraswati and the sage underlines the importance of guidance and wisdom in our inner journey. It's not uncommon for us to be blinded by our daily roles and routines, losing sight of the light of our Aatman, the eternal soul. The sage acts as a mirror, reflecting and reminding Saraswati of her true nature, showing us that sometimes it takes an outside eye to recognize our inner light.

Saraswati's realization that she is a complete and perfect expression of the divine is a powerful revelation. It demonstrates that understanding our Aatman doesn't require an external quest or radical transformation; it's already present within us. Each individual is a unique reflection of universal consciousness, and by recognizing this, we can live with deeper harmony and peace, knowing that we are intrinsically linked to all that exists.

24. THE WIND AND ARJUNA

Dharma leadership

In ancient times, Arjuna, the great warrior of the Mahabharata, stood atop a hill, contemplating the vast expanse of land that opened up before him. His heart was heavy with doubts about the battle ahead and about dharma, his sacred duty. The clouds of uncertainty clouded his mind, just as they veiled the sky above.

As he stood there, frozen in thought, a powerful wind began to blow. This was no ordinary wind, but one that seemed to carry the whispers of the ancients and the wisdom of the world itself. Arjuna closed his eyes, letting the wind blow through him, and listened.

"Why do you trouble yourself, Arjuna?" whispered the wind in a voice that seemed to come from everywhere and nowhere at once.

Arjuna opened his eyes in astonishment. "Who are you?" he asked.

"I am the wind, the one who roams the earth without attachment, the one who follows his own path without question, the one who is the manifestation of Vayu, the god of wind," replied the voice. "Why then, Arjuna, is a warrior of your stature as motionless as stone when his path is as clear as day?"

"I'm afraid of going wrong with my dharma, of taking a path that would lead to misfortune and destruction," Arjuna confessed with humility.

The wind blew around Arjuna in a whirlwind, and in this movement, Arjuna saw scenes from his past life, the choices he had made, and the consequences of these choices. The wind spoke without words, showing that each action led to the next, that nothing was still, just as he himself never stopped moving.

"Arjuna," the wind resumed, its voice now soft as a breeze, "your dharma is like my direction. I don't question where I'm going; I simply follow my nature. You're a warrior, a protector of justice and goodness. To follow your dharma is to follow your nature, and that can never be wrong."

Arjuna felt a clarity come over him. He understood that just as the wind never doubted its direction, he too had to be sure in his action, unhindered by fear of the consequences. His dharma was to fight for goodness and fairness, no matter what the obstacles.

With this revelation, the wind died down, leaving Arjuna alone on the hill. The warrior knew what he had to do. He descended the hill with unshakeable resolve, ready to face his destiny.

In the days that followed, Arjuna led his companions into battle with renewed courage, guided by the firmness of his dharma. And while the winds of war blew around him, he remained steadfast, a pillar of determination and honor, teaching all that the true direction of life is that dictated by our deepest nature and sacred duty.

The Infallibility of Inner Duty

Arjuna's lesson on the hill teaches us that doubt is often a greater obstacle than the trial itself. Like the wind, which does not question its path, we are invited to listen to our inner essence to find our direction. The warrior understands that his dharma is inherent and unshakeable, emphasizing that fidelity to our true nature and roles is essential to moving forward with confidence and integrity in life.

Arjuna's vision, illuminated by the wisdom of the wind, illustrates the importance of clarity of purpose in our existence. The wind, an incarnation of Vayu, shows that every element of creation follows its own dharma without hesitation. It reminds us that when we are lost, we must seek answers in alignment with our deepest duty, for therein lies our most reliable moral compass.

Ultimately, Arjuna's story is a testament to the strength that comes from adhering to one's own dharma. By committing himself unreservedly to the battle destined for him, Arjuna becomes a symbol of courage and honor. His determination reminds us that, in the face of life's storms, standing firm in our convictions and acting in accordance with our sacred duty is the noblest of paths.

25. THE SWAN AND ADVAITA

Duality in unity

In an ancient Indian kingdom, there lived an immaculately white swan who spent his days gliding majestically over the shimmering waters of a vast lake. This swan, named Hamsa, was known among all creatures for his beauty and grace. But Hamsa was looking for something deeper than the superficial compliments he received; he was looking for an understanding of Advaita, the principle of non-duality that proclaims everything in the universe to be one and indivisible.

One day, as Hamsa was meditating under the gentle sun, he heard the voice of an invisible sage. "Hamsa, you seek to understand Advaita, but you look outside for what can only be found within yourself," the voice said.

Astonished but intrigued, Hamsa replied, "How can I understand Advaita, when I see around me so many forms, so much diversity?"

The voice replied: "Plunge into the depths of your being and rise above appearances. What is below is like what is above. You sail the waters, separated between heaven and the deep, but aren't you also a part of both worlds?"

Inspired by these words, Hamsa dived deep beneath the waters of the lake, where silence reigned and sunlight barely filtered through the waves. In these depths, Hamsa no longer felt the boundary between the water and his own being. He felt a unity with the element that surrounded him, a sense that he was one with the water.

As he rose to the surface, he looked up at the sky and took to the air. In the heavens, he flew so high that the waters of the lake were but a distant mirror. And there, among the clouds, he felt the same unity with the air, an absence of boundaries, a wholeness.

"You see, Hamsa," the sage's voice resumed, "as you are one with water and air, all is one in the essence of Advaita. Duality is only a perception, an illusion born of ignorance."

Hamsa pondered these words and realized that, just as he was swan, water and air, every element in the universe carried within it the essence of everything else. Separation was just an illusion, for at the deepest level, everything was connected.

With this understanding, Hamsa became a guide for other creatures, teaching by example the truth of Advaita. He glided over the waters not just as a swan, but as a master who saw beyond the illusions of separation and lived every moment in full awareness of the unity of all existence.

And so, Hamsa's story spread far beyond the borders of his lake, becoming a timeless tale, a reminder that in the teeming diversity of life lies a simple and profound truth: we are all manifestations of the same divine essence, and in this recognition lies ultimate peace and freedom.

The Essence of Unity

Hamsa's journey teaches us that the truth of unity lies beyond appearances. In the quest for Advaita, the swan discovers that perceived duality is merely an illusion, a superficiality that masks the intrinsic interconnectedness of all existence. This fable invites us to look beyond our limited perceptions and seek understanding in the very essence of our being, where the ultimate truth of universal unity lies.

By plunging into the depths and ascending to the heights, Hamsa directly experiences this non-duality. He embodies the maxim "What's below is like what's above", demonstrating that our essence is uniform across various states of existence. This tale illustrates that understanding the fundamental unity of the universe is an inner journey, an awakening to the continuity between self and cosmos.

Ultimately, Hamsa's story stands as a powerful symbol of Advaitic wisdom, reminding us that every being, every element of nature, carries the essence of everything else. Recognizing this truth frees us from the shackles of separation, opening the way to a deeper harmony with the world around us and within us. By discovering our indivisible link with the whole of creation, we find a peace and freedom that transcend the illusions of diversity.

26. Fire and Bhakti

Fiery devotion

In a small, prosperous town bordered by fields of lotus flowers and mango trees, lived a young girl named Anika. She possessed a boundless curiosity for the mysteries of the world, but often found herself perplexed by the rituals and devotional practices of her elders. To her, the flames of the yagnas (sacred fires) were mere flickering lights, and the mantras recited seemed like empty whispers against the immensity of the sky.

On the eve of the great Navaratri festival, Anika approached the old village priestess, a wise woman known as Maa Kamala, who was preparing the fire for the evening ritual. "Maa Kamala, how can fire connect us to the gods? How can the repetition of words be the key to devotion?" she asked.

Maa Kamala, with a gentle smile and a twinkle in her eye, invited Anika to take part in the ritual preparation. "To understand bhakti, you have to feel it, not just ask questions about it. Prepare the fire with me," she said.

Anika agreed, intrigued. Together, they gathered sandalwood branches and dried flowers, and arranged fruit and ghee offerings around the fire. The sun began to decline, and the first sparks were lit. The flames came to life, dancing on the fragrant wood, and Anika lost herself in their hypnotic ballet.

"Sing with me," invited Maa Kamala. The mantras Anika had heard so many times took on a new form, as if each syllable were a breath of life for the flames. The old priestess's words seemed to feed the fire, and as they sang, the warmth of the blaze enveloped Anika, not only on her skin but in her heart too.

As night fell and the stars came out, Anika felt a growing warmth, not the heat of the flame, but an inner warmth. She realized that bhakti was not just about deeds or words, but about total surrender to the moment, in the purity of the heart that accepts divine light.

The singing continued, and Anika, for the first time, shed tears not of sadness, but of deep, overflowing joy. The other villagers joined them, forming a circle around the fire, and although she was the youngest, Anika felt equal to them all, united by the flame of devotion.

When the ritual ended and the fire was reduced to glowing embers, Anika turned to Maa Kamala, her eyes shining with understanding. "I feel the bhakti, Maa," she murmured. "It was there all the time, waiting for me to open my heart."

Maa Kamala nodded with satisfaction. "Bhakti is like that fire, Anika. It has to be lit and fed. And once it burns within you, it lights up everything in its path."

The night came to an end, but for Anika, a new path was opening up, a path of inner light and warmth, of devotion and love. And every time she saw a flame afterwards, she remembered that night when she'd learned that true devotion was a fire that never goes out, a fire that warms the soul and lights the way.

The Inner Flame of Devotion

Anika's quest to understand bhakti reveals that devotion is not mere adherence to external rituals, but an inner flame that needs to be lit and nurtured. Anika's transformation shows that devotion is a path of personal discovery, where symbols and rituals become meaningful only when we engage with them with an open and receptive heart. True bhakti is therefore a lived experience, a spiritual awakening that manifests itself in the warm embrace of faith.

By actively participating in the fire ritual, Anika discovers that devotional practices are vehicles that transport the soul to a deeper understanding. Bhakti becomes an act of love and reception, where the repetition of mantras and the illumination of flames transcend their materiality to become expressions of a greater truth. It is in the surrender to these acts that the divine is perceived, illuminating the path of wisdom with the light of pure devotion.

27. The Desert and Moksha

The thirst for liberation

In the arid expanses of Thar, a traveler named Vidur walked, his footsteps drawing fleeting imprints in the fine sand. The sweltering heat of the sun formed mirages on the horizon, where sky and earth melted into illusions of water. Vidur sought Moksha, liberation from the incessant cycle of life and death, but in this hostile environment, his quest seemed in vain. All he found were endless dunes and a merciless sun.

Daylight fell, replaced by an inky night dotted with stars, bringing relative coolness. Vidur, exhausted, sat down and looked up at the sky. The constellations told him stories of gods and distant worlds. As he contemplated the immensity, a feeling of peace came over him. He realized that Moksha was not a place to be reached, but a state of being, a detachment not only from earthly pleasures and sufferings, but also from expectations and desires.

Suddenly, a swirl of sand rose up in front of him, and through this dancing veil, a shape took shape. It was neither man nor animal, but a desert spirit as old as time. "Why do you seek Moksha in this lifeless desert, traveler?" the spirit asked in a voice as gentle as the breath of the wind.

"To escape the cycle of suffering," replied Vidur.

The spirit laughs softly. "Suffering and pleasure are like those dunes, always moving, changing place but never nature. Moksha is the understanding that you are neither the dune nor the wind, but the space between them."

Vidur meditated on these words. He understood that Moksha was the space of consciousness in which he stood, an impassive witness to the ephemeral spectacle of creation. As dawn tinted the sky gold and pink, the spirit vanished as suddenly as it had appeared, leaving Vidur alone with the revelation of his true nature.

The traveler remained in the desert for several days, each grain of sand teaching him patience, each star reminding him of his small place in the universe. When he finally left the Thar, he was no longer a man seeking liberation, but a free being, carrying within him the peace of the desert, the serenity of the starry skies, and the wisdom of the wind spirit.

His thirst for Moksha was quenched, not by a mirage oasis, but by the profound knowledge that liberation comes from within, from the acceptance that all is ephemeral, except the space of quietude deep within the soul. Vidur shared his story with all those seeking peace, teaching them that the desert of life, with its illusions and mirages, could become the cradle of eternal liberation.

The Inner Oasis of Wisdom

Vidur's quest across the dunes of the Thar teaches us that liberation is not to be found in the conquest of an external place or the attainment of a material goal, but in the understanding and acceptance of the ephemeral nature of existence. His realization that Moksha is an internal state of being, a peaceful detachment from the illusion of extremes, illuminates the true essence of freedom. Peace lies not in the absence of suffering, but in inner balance and tranquillity in the face of the inevitable waves of pleasure and pain.

Vidur's encounter with the desert spirit symbolizes a crucial realization: we are not the transient events of our lives, but the unchanging witnesses who observe them. This realization reveals that liberation comes from within, from a space of awareness where we recognize that external reality is in perpetual change, and that our true essence is constant and unalterable.

Finally, Vidur's experience shows that every moment of life can be a teacher on the path to Moksha, if we welcome each experience with patience and understanding. True liberation is an acceptance of the eternal dance between creation and dissolution, and peace comes from knowing that the oasis of wisdom is already within us, an inner refuge where the eternal resides.

28. The Squirrel and the Ramayana

Small actions and their impact

In the vast canopy of the Dandaka forest, a little squirrel named Mani frolicked between the trees. His days were filled with small quests: finding nuts, playing with his friends, and marvelling at the beauty of nature. Mani, however, carried within him an unquenchable desire to contribute to something great, something that would surpass the limits of his small existence.

One day, as the sun poured its warmth over the land, an unusual commotion shook the forest. Mani climbed to the top of a tree and saw a sight that fascinated him: armies of monkeys and bears were busy building a bridge to the island of Lanka. It was the army of the valiant Rama, on a mission to rescue Sita, the divine wife kidnapped by the demon Ravana.

Mani timidly approached the construction frenzy. He saw gigantic creatures carrying heavy rocks and throwing them into the ocean. The little squirrel, filled with an ardent will, decided to help this noble cause. He dived into the water, rolled in the fine sand, and shook his little body over the rocks, making the sand stick to them, hoping this would help bind them together.

At first, nobody noticed Mani's tiny efforts. But after a while, Rama himself observed the little animal's determination. Touched by his devotion and commitment, he approached Mani. With a benevolent smile, he gently stroked the squirrel's back with his finger, leaving three lines - a blessing that would mark the squirrels forever.

Mani's action, however small, inspired all those working on deck. They saw that no contribution was too small, and that every effort, when made with a sincere heart, has its place in the grand design of the universe.

The bridge was completed with everyone's help, and Rama was able to cross and finally defeat Ravana, freeing Sita. The legend of Mani spread far beyond the forests of Dandaka, becoming an eternal symbol that even the most modest action is essential to the triumph of good.

The Dandaka forest sang the epic of the Ramayana, and in this melody, we could also hear the soft, determined note of Mani, the squirrel who had dared to believe in the importance of his participation. And for every squirrel who would henceforth bear the marks of Rama, it would be a reminder that greatness often lies in the sum of all small deeds.

The Echo of Simple Gestures

The story of Mani, the squirrel, conveys a powerful truth: no action, no matter how small, is insignificant when performed with a pure heart and sincere intention. Mani's participation in the building of the bridge reminds us that every effort counts, and that the success of an undertaking often depends on the sum of many modest contributions, rather than a few gigantic deeds.

Rama's acknowledgement of Mani's effort underlines the importance of appreciation and recognition. It teaches us that the value of an action is not measured by its immediate impact, but by the intention and perseverance behind it. The story illustrates that acts of courage and devotion, no matter how small, can inspire others and send out a shockwave of positive effort.

Finally, the legend of the squirrel in the Ramayana is a tribute to the lasting impact of small actions. It reminds us that we are all capable of leaving a positive mark on the world. Mani's story is a call to act with determination and hope, motivating us to do our part in the great epic of life, because every well-intentioned gesture contributes to the fabric of a better future.

29. The Turtle and Yoga

Anchored in the present

In the peaceful land of Bharat, in the heart of the vast green expanse bordering the Ganges, lived a turtle named Kachhapa. She had a reputation for being as wise as she was ancient, wearing the scars of time on her shell like medals of honor. However, despite her wisdom, Kachhapa often felt disconnected, as if every moment was slipping through her clutches before she could fully experience it.

One morning, as dawn painted the sky in shades of pink and gold, Kachhapa decided to venture out of her usual seclusion. As she slowly made her way towards the river's sacred spring, she came across a group of ascetics. They were motionless, completely absorbed in strange and complex postures, balancing their bodies in ways that defied the turtle's comprehension.

Kachhapa observed with curiosity these human beings who seemed so intensely present, so deeply anchored in the moment, that they were like living statues. One of the ascetics, noticing her interest, approached her after her practice and sat down beside her.

"You seem intrigued by our practice, wise turtle," he said with a smile.

"Indeed," replied Kachhapa. "I'm trying to understand how to stay anchored in the present, how to capture every moment."

The ascetic, a yogi named Patanjali, gently replied: "Yoga is the dance of every cell with the light of day, where every breath is a musical note and every movement a harmony. It is the art of living each moment to the full."

"Could I learn?" asked Kachhapa, his eyes shining with sincere desire.

Thus began the teaching of Kachhapa. Patanjali adapted it to the turtle's unique abilities. First, she learned to breathe consciously, following her own slow, measured rhythm.

Then she began with simple postures, extensions that respected the natural curve of her shell.

With each posture, Kachhapa felt her mind becoming more stable, her concentration sharpening. She learned the turtle posture, Kurmasana, which enabled her to withdraw into her inner self, exploring the depths of her being. She also mastered the stable, balanced posture called the Mountain, where she stood motionless, feeling the firmness of the earth beneath her.

As the days and months went by, the practice of Kachhapa transformed not only her mind, but also her relationship with the world around her. Every leaf that fell, every raindrop that hit her shell, every breeze that caressed her face was a whole universe she could explore.

Kachhapa became a symbol of tranquility and presence for the creatures of the forest. Birds came to perch on her shell, fish glided slowly by her side when she meditated in the water, and even the trees seemed to bow gently in her presence.

Yoga had taught her that every moment is an eternity in itself, and that anchoring oneself in the present is the most precious of wisdoms. Kachhapa, the yogi turtle, thus found her place, not in stretching towards what had not yet arrived, or in retracting from what had been, but in fully embracing the present moment.

The Embrace of the Instant

Kachhapa's quest to live in the moment reveals the essence of contentment. By embracing the teachings of yoga, the turtle shows us that fulfillment lies in our ability to anchor ourselves in the present moment. It is in the awareness of our breath and the acceptance of our natural rhythm that we can truly experience the richness of each moment.

Kachhapa's transformation into a creature of tranquility underlines the power of constancy and patience. By applying herself to a practice suited to her essence, she discovers that stillness can be as rich in experience as the most dynamic movement. This revelation is an invitation to seek our own path to inner stability, recognizing that complete immersion in the present is the true journey.

30. HEAVEN AND SAMSARA

The immensity of the life cycle

In a remote village on the great Indian subcontinent, an exhausted traveler named Devraj stopped for the night. He had just crossed dense forests, noisy towns and turbulent rivers. That evening, the firmament shone with a rare intensity, a mosaic of light dappled through the veil of darkness.

Devraj lay on his back, contemplating the immensity of the heavens, when suddenly it seemed as if the stars began to whisper to him. It was as if the sky itself had been transformed into an ancient storyteller, whose timbre was as gentle as the night wind and as deep as the echo of sacred caves.

"Listen, son of Earth," whispered Heaven, "for I'm about to reveal to you the secret of Samsara, the endless cycle of birth, life, death and rebirth."

Devraj, intrigued and somewhat skeptical, nevertheless decided to lend an ear to the celestial sayings. "How can I understand this infinite cycle? I'm just a weary traveler in search of rest," he replied.

"Look at these stars," the sky continued, "Each light you see is a passage, a tale of a soul on its way through Samsara. Some shine brightly, living a life of splendor and joy, while others flicker dimly, carrying the burden of their lessons to be learned."

Devraj, staring into the glittering abyss, saw shooting stars crossing the firmament and fading away. "And what happens to those that fall?" he asked.

"These souls have completed a cycle. They rest before being reborn, transformed by the experiences they have acquired. Like them, you are traversing your own path through Samsara. Every joy and trial you endure is but a step towards ultimate understanding."

The sky then paused, allowing silence to envelop the traveler, who was gradually assimilating this wisdom. "And how can I free myself from this cycle?" murmured Devraj, his voice filled with a mixture of awe and reverence.

"By living each life with intention and understanding, seeking Dharma, the universal law, and fulfilling your Karma without attachment to the fruits of your actions. Thus, gradually, you will come closer to Moksha, final liberation."

The sky seemed to be coming closer, enveloping Devraj in an astral embrace, offering him an unexpected sense of peace.

"Samsara is vast like me, yet at its heart it contains a simplicity that every soul can grasp. Live fully, love freely, learn humbly, and let go gracefully."

As the hours wore on, the sky's words faded into the dawn haze. When Devraj awoke, the rising sun was painting the sky gold and purple. He rose, his heart lightened, carrying with him the tranquility of infinite space and the echo of the stars. He now knew that every step, every breath, every moment of his life was part of the vast and magnificent Samsara. And with this knowledge, he resumed his journey, a soul among the stars, walking the path of understanding.

The Inner Journey Towards Understanding

The wisdom shared by the heavens at Devraj reveals a universal truth about human existence: each life is a chapter in the great book of Samsara. Like stars in the night, our lives are sparks in the immensity of the cosmos, each following its own path, illuminated by its own joys and sorrows. This celestial metaphor reminds us that our passage on earth, however mysterious and ephemeral, carries with it the potential for learning and transformation.

The fall of a star, far from being an end, symbolizes rest and rebirth, offering a comforting perspective on our own endings and beginnings. Devraj understands that the challenges he encounters are merely steps towards greater fulfillment. He thus teaches us that acceptance of life's cycles, with their ups and downs, is crucial to fully embracing our personal journey.

Living with intention, acting without attachment, and seeking wisdom in every experience brings us closer to Moksha, liberation. It's a call to walk the earth with a celestial perspective, where every choice and every act is guided by the search for harmony with the universe.

31. The Sun and Brahman

Universal enlightenment

In a forgotten corner of India, where rivers whisper ancient secrets and trees sway to the rhythm of eternal truths, lived a sage named Aarav. This sage, known for his great erudition, spent his days meditating on the nature of Brahman, the ultimate, omnipresent essence of the universe.

One morning, as dawn caressed the horizon, Aarav sat beneath the great banyan tree, eyes closed, heart open, seeking to perceive the presence of Brahman in the breeze, in the birdsong, in the rustling of the leaves. Yet a sense of frustration gripped him. Despite his deep meditations, Brahman always seemed just out of reach, an insoluble enigma, an elusive presence. It was then that the sun, in its celestial course, stopped for a moment above him. Its light penetrated the canopy of trees and bathed Aarav in a soft, comforting warmth.

"Sage Aarav," said the sun in his radiant voice, "why do you seek Brahman as one seeks a pearl in the ocean?"

Aarav, astonished to be addressing the sun itself, humbly replied, "O Light of the world, I seek to recognize Brahman in everything, but I find this quest more arduous than I expected."

The sun shone brighter and said, "Look around you, Aarav. What do you see?"

Aarav opened his eyes and saw the world bathed in light. He saw the leaves of the banyan tree glitter like precious stones, he saw the water of the river sparkle like a mirror of infinity, he saw the petals of the lotus flowers open to life.

"I see the beauty of the world, I see creation in all its splendor," murmured Aarav.

"What you see is my essence projected onto the world. Without me, there would be no color, no form, no life. I am in everything and everything is in me. So it is with Brahman," explained the sun.

The sage, absorbing these words, felt a veil lift from his heart. "So Brahman is not only in the inner search but also in the appreciation of the outer, in the recognition of the divine essence in everything?"

"Precisely," smiled the sun. "The light I spread is but a reflection of this truth. Brahman is in every ray that caresses the Earth, in every life I nourish. It is the recognition of this truth that is universal enlightenment."

The sun resumed its course, leaving Aarav alone with this revelation. From then on, every morning, when the sun raised its golden torch above the world, Aarav greeted its light and saw Brahman in the flight of a butterfly, in the curve of a river, in the smile of a child.

And in this new understanding, Aarav found the enlightenment he had so long sought, knowing that Brahman was neither distant nor alien, but a loving presence in all things, the inner light that connects everything in the universe.

The Light of Universal Consciousness

Aarav's quest teaches us that enlightenment is not found in isolated asceticism or solitary contemplation, but in conscious connection with the world around us. The wisdom of the sun reveals to him that the divine presence, Brahman, is an underlying fabric of all creation, perceptible in the simplicity and splendor of nature. This story is a reminder that spirituality does not exclude the sensory world, but embraces it, recognizing the divine in the everyday.

The sage's revelation under the banyan tree illustrates that true enlightenment lies not in the conquest of abstract knowledge, but in the ability to see and appreciate the manifestation of the sacred in every aspect of life. It is in the wonder of sunlight, the beauty of lotus flowers and the grace of a butterfly's flight that Brahman is revealed. What we long for often lies in the simple brilliance of the world around us.

Enlightenment is not a distant state to be attained, but an intimate understanding that everything is interconnected, that every ray of light, every child's smile carries within it the spark of the universal. By opening up to this vision, we find peace and wisdom in the unity of all existence.

32. THE MOUNTAIN AND THE DETACHMENT

Unchangeability in the face of change

In a lost valley, where the echoes of ancient Vedic chants seem to whisper through the winds, stood the mountain of Dhairya, a peak as immutable as it was awe-inspiring. At its foot, a hermit named Vimal had established his dwelling, a simple shelter made of branches and leaves, seeking peace in the eternal solitude of the stones.

Vimal, once a prince among men, had left everything behind to find serenity in detachment. However, the hermit was still battling the inner storms of his former desires and attachments. He longed for the stability of the mountain, which remained unshakeable in the face of seasons and centuries.

One night, as the moon bathed the world in silvery light, Dhairya Mountain came to life before Vimal's astonished eyes. With a voice as deep as the distant rumble of a thunderstorm, she spoke:

"Vimal, why is your heart as tumultuous as the river flows below?"

Vimal reverently replied, "O great Dhairya, I seek to be unchanging like you, free from all desire, but I find it as difficult as holding the wind between my fingers."

"The wind, rivers, creatures and even mountains, everything changes, transforms and passes," says the mountain. "To be unchanging does not mean to be without movement or change, but rather to witness these changes without becoming attached to them."

Intrigued, Vimal asked how he could reach this state.

"Observe," said Dhairya. The mountain then showed Vimal visions of the world: civilizations rising and falling, rivers changing course, forests growing and deserts spreading.

"Everything that has a form changes. It's the law of nature. Your body, your thoughts, your feelings, they're like these visions, constantly changing. Detachment comes from understanding that you are not these ephemeral things. You are the witness to these changes."

At these words, Vimal contemplated the mountain and realized that, although its outer form had remained unchanged over the eons, inside it was the scene of perpetual change: rocks metamorphosed, ecosystems were born and died. It was the dance of creation and destruction, visible to those who knew how to look.

"The mountain you see today is not the same as yesterday, and yet it is. So, although you change, your true essence remains. That's detachment," concludes Dhairya.

With this understanding, Vimal spent the next few days in deep meditation, observing the changes in and around him without judgment or the desire to hold on to anything. He saw his thoughts and emotions as clouds passing in the sky of his consciousness, without attaching himself to them, without pursuing them.

In this way, Vimal discovered the wisdom of the mountain within himself: immutability in the face of change, peace in the acceptance that all is ephemeral except the silent witness of experience - the inner presence that is in harmony with the whole.

Serenity in Impermanence

The lesson Vimal receives from Dhairya Mountain is a powerful reminder of the transitory nature of existence. Detachment doesn't come from isolation or indifference to the world, but from a deep understanding that everything tangible is subject to change. This awareness is the first step towards genuine inner peace, where we are no longer buffeted by the storms of desires and attachments.

In his quest for stability, Vimal discovers that immutability is not the absence of movement, but constancy in the observation of change. The wisdom of the mountains reveals to him that, just as natural landscapes change gracefully, so man can remain inwardly unperturbed by life's metamorphoses. True tranquility lies in the recognition that our essence remains unchanged despite the ceaseless flow of forms around us.

33. THE HARE AND THE MAYA

The illusion of fear

In the deep forest of Chandanavana, where every tree seems to tell an ancient story, lived a hare named Chandra. Chandra was known among the forest animals for his trembling heart, for he was frightened by the shadow and rustle of every leaf. His mind was a kaleidoscope of fears and anxieties, making him a slave to his own illusions.

One evening, as the round, luminous moon rose into the sky, Chandra was startled by a powerful sound. The sound, resounding like the drum of the earth, was none other than thunder following a silvery flash that ripped through the sky. The hare, convinced that the end of the world had arrived, zigzagged through the forest, howling in terror.

His panic was contagious, and soon a tide of forest creatures followed him, amplifying the cacophony of shrieks and squeaks. They ran until they reached a clear, peaceful lake, home to a wise flamingo known as Jnana.

Jnana, with her peaceful pink feathers and penetrating eyes, looked at the tide of frightened animals and addressed Chandra: "Why this panic, little hare? What is the source of this terror that has disturbed Chandanavana's quietude?"

Chandra, panting and trembling, replied, "O wise Jnana, the earth is cracking, the world is ending, and we are fleeing for our lives."

The flamingo, knowing the capricious nature of fear, simply said, "Show me where the earth cracks."

Together they returned to the spot where Chandra had heard the terrifying sound. Jnana, with unruffled calm, examined the scene and, seeing a fallen and cracked coconut, revealed the true source of the noise.

"Chandra," said the flamingo, "what you heard was just the sound of that coconut falling from the sky. It was your mind that turned this mundane incident into a catastrophe."

The confused hare looked at the flamingo with pleading eyes.

"You live in Maya, the cosmic illusion," Jnana explained. "Your fears, too, are part of this great illusion. They are born of your thoughts and feed on your attention. If you give them less importance, they will lose their hold on you."

Jnana then invited Chandra to sit by the lake and observe the waves created by the raindrops. "Like these waves, your fears come and go. They are not you. If you learn to observe your fears without attaching your heart to them, they will lose their power."

With time, Chandra learned to remain calm, to observe his fears as he observed waves on water, with detachment and wisdom. He understood that his fears, though seemingly real, were illusions, shadows of reality, creations of his own mind.

The forest of Chandanavana regained its peace, and Chandra, the hare, lived there in harmony, no longer a slave to his fears, but master of his mind, recognizing that fear, like everything else in Maya, was a veil over the truth, a veil he could now lift.

The Illusory Shadow of Fear

The fable of Chandra the hare reveals the mind's tendency to weave alternate realities out of simple incidents. Fears, often unfounded, can become tyrannical masters, disturbing our inner peace and causing unnecessary chaos. It's a reminder of how our distorted perceptions can set off chain reactions, not only in ourselves but also in those around us.

Chandra's encounter with the wise flamingo, Jnana, highlights the need for calm introspection to distinguish reality from illusion. The flamingo teaches that fear loses its hold when we face it with clear awareness and put it in its proper place, as a passing phenomenon rather than an absolute truth. This awareness is essential to regaining our balance in the tumult of frightening circumstances.

This story invites us to recognize that, even in the face of life's noises and shadows, we have the power to choose serenity over panic, and so lift the veil of Maya to see the light of truth.

34. The Moon and the Rishi

The phases of knowledge

In the vast expanse of India, where the night sky reveals itself in all its splendor, a rishi by the name of Devadas lived in a modest hut on the edge of a village. He was known not only for his wisdom, but also for his incessant quest for knowledge. Every night, Devadas would sit outside his home and meditate under the moonlight, seeking to understand the mysteries of the universe.

One night, when the moon was full and bright, Devadas fell into a meditation so deep that he felt his spirit rise above the limits of his body. In this trance, he addressed a prayer to the moon, asking it to reveal to him the secret of absolute knowledge.

To his surprise, the moon answered him. She said, "O Devadas, you seek knowledge as if it were a destination to be reached, but that's not how wisdom works. Like me, it goes through phases and seasons."

The moon continued, "Look how I change shape. I'm new, then I grow until I'm full, then I shrink again. Each phase is necessary, and none is permanent. Likewise, the knowledge you seek is not a static entity. It evolves, grows with experience, and sometimes fades away to make room for new perspectives."

The moon shone brightly as she revealed her teaching. "The new moon is like ignorance, where knowledge is hidden. But that's just the beginning. The waxing moon is like learning, where each night brings more light and understanding. When I'm full, knowledge is complete, but it's not finished. For it must retreat again, leaving you in darkness, so that you can appreciate and reflect on the light you've received."

Devadas listened, absorbing every word. He realized that his efforts to find complete knowledge were like trying to grasp the full moon every night. It was impossible, because the very nature of knowledge is to change and renew itself, just like the phases of the moon.

The days passed, and with each night Devadas meditated under the changing phases of the moon, learning to accept uncertainty and find wisdom in the cycles of growth and decline. He learned that sometimes you had to live in darkness to understand the value of light, and that complete knowledge was an ever-shifting horizon.

Rishi Devadas became a symbol of wisdom for the villagers, not because he had all the answers, but because he understood the value of questions and the power of humility in the quest for wisdom. He taught that, like the moon, true knowledge is never full or empty, but always in transformation, always in phase with the great cycle of life.

The Wisdom of Eternal Cycles

The parable of Devadas and the moon offers us a profound metaphor for the pursuit of knowledge. It teaches us that wisdom is not a summit to be conquered, but a journey through ceaseless cycles of learning and discovery. The moon's response illuminates this truth: knowledge is dynamic, evolving, and never crystallizes into an ultimate or complete form.

The moon, with its ever-changing phases, symbolizes the ephemeral nature of intellectual enlightenment. Each phase of the moon represents a stage of understanding that must be accepted and integrated. The full moon of knowledge can be eclipsed, reminding us that completeness is often followed by a period of withdrawal necessary for integration and reflection, paving the way for new cycles of growth.

This story invites us to embrace humility in the quest for knowledge, and to recognize that every moment of ignorance is a prelude to potential knowledge. Accepting that complete understanding is an ever-evolving horizon allows us to live with an ever-renewed curiosity and appreciation for the process, as much as for the revelations it brings.

35. Forest and Dharma

The natural harmony of duties

In a faraway kingdom, bordered by a dense, ancient forest, lived a young prince named Arjun. From an early age, he was tormented by questions of duty and dharma. One day, determined to find the answers to his torments, Arjun set off alone into the forest, leaving behind the advice of his tutors and the echoes of the royal court.

No sooner had he entered the canopy than he was greeted by the murmur of leaves and the song of streams. Here, far from the complexity of human laws, every creature seemed to lead an existence defined by an invisible harmony.

Arjun first observed an ant, busily carrying a load far too heavy for its small size. "Why do you toil like that?" he asked. The ant stopped and replied: "It's my dharma, Prince. To carry, to work, to contribute to the community. That's the role I've been given, and I embrace it fully."

The prince, intrigued, continued his quest for knowledge and then encountered a majestic peacock, displaying its feathers in a burst of color. "Why this parade?" asked Arjun. "It's my dharma," explained the peacock. "To exhibit my beauty, to embody the splendor of creation and thus inspire those who look upon me."

As Arjun advanced, each encounter revealed a different aspect of dharma. The tiger hunted gracefully, honoring its role as predator. The tree offered shade and fruit, satisfying its nurturing nature. Even the snake, often feared and despised, did its part by regulating rodent populations.

Lost in thought, Arjun sat down at the foot of a large banyan, the king tree of the forest. He felt humbled by this natural harmony, where every creature, big or small, followed its path without question.

It was then that the banyan came to life and addressed him: "Prince Arjun, you seek to understand dharma as if it were unique and identical for everyone. But look around you: every living being has its own dharma, an innate path dictated by its nature and essence. The forest is in balance because each one fulfils its role without coveting that of another."

Arjun realized that dharma was not a burden to be carried, but a natural expression of self. The dharma of a prince was not that of an ant, nor that of a peacock, but it was just as essential to the order of the world.

Returning to the palace, Arjun no longer sought to imitate the duty of others or to conform to some abstract idea of dharma.

He pledged to govern with justice, compassion and wisdom, encouraging everyone to find and follow their own path. For he had understood, thanks to the forest, that harmony is born when each being embraces its unique dharma and contributes to the symphony of life.

The Essence of Being and Universal Harmony

Arjun's quest through the forest illustrates a universal truth about the nature of dharma, revealing that each being has a unique role to play in the great orchestra of life. This diversity of duties, far from being a source of confusion or conflict, is the keystone of natural harmony. History teaches us that our dharma is not an imposed burden, but an authentic expression of our essence.

As the wisdom of the forest shows, seeking to imitate the role of another leads to dissonance, while accepting our own path brings balance. Each creature, by embracing its own dharma, contributes to the stability of the whole. Arjun discovers that peace comes from understanding our unique place in the world and honoring it through our actions.

The final lesson is one of self-acceptance and recognition of the intrinsic value of each role in society. True harmony, as in the forest, is achieved when we align our actions with the deepest nature of our being, allowing the collective symphony to flourish in all its diversity and beauty.

36. The Lake and Reflection

The mirror of the soul

In an ancient village, carved between the folds of the Himalayas, lived a wise man named Devan. He was known for his wisdom and calm, qualities that made him a guide and advisor to all. But Devan, for all his knowledge, was still seeking clarity on the true essence of the soul.

One dawn, as the sky turned orange and pink, Devan walked to a sacred lake nestled between the mountains. The water was so clear and calm that it seemed like a piece of heaven fallen to earth. The villagers believed that this lake was a window to the divine, capable of reflecting the truth of the soul of whoever looked into it.

Devan sat down on the shore and watched his reflection. He saw not only her face, wrinkled with age, but also the sparkle of life in her eyes, which seemed to dance with the morning light. For hours, he remained motionless, his gaze immersed in the mirror of the water, seeking to see beyond his physical image.

As the sun reached its zenith, Devan had an epiphany. His reflection began to ripple, the wrinkles on his face mingling with the ripples in the water. He saw in himself kings and beggars, mountains and rivers, stars and galaxies. He understood that his soul was not an isolated entity but a reflection of the cosmos itself, diverse and constantly evolving.

He realized that what he was looking for was not outside but inside himself. The truth of the soul was like the water in the lake - clear and tranquil, reflecting all that is without adhering to it, deep beyond what the eyes can see.

Devan spent many days by the lake, feeding his mind with this new understanding. When he returned to the village, his teaching had changed. He no longer spoke of soul-searching as an external quest, but as the discovery of the universe itself.

The villagers began to understand that each soul is a calm lake, capable of reflecting the world in all its complexity and beauty. Peace, Devan taught them, comes from the ability to observe our reflection without disturbing the water, to see the truth of our soul without the veil of illusions.

And so, the lake became a sacred place not only for Devan, but for all those who sought to understand the depths of their own being. They learned that the soul, like the lake, reflects the light of knowledge and wisdom when it is calm and peaceful.

The story of Devan and the sacred lake spread beyond the mountains, teaching future generations that every being possesses within itself a mirror capable of revealing the deepest truth. And this mirror is inner silence, the peace that comes when we accept the reflection of our own soul.

The Inner Lake: Self-revelation

Devan's odyssey by the sacred lake teaches a valuable lesson about the nature of the soul and the search for wisdom. The surface of the lake, like a mirror, symbolizes our ability to reflect the complexity of the cosmos within us. This story reminds us that clarity comes from introspection and inner calm, not from external pursuit. It invites us to recognize that each individual holds within him or herself an entire universe, a reflection of the infinite that deserves to be explored with reverence.

The wise Devan, contemplating his reflection on the still water, reveals that self-understanding is intrinsic and that the soul reveals its truth when observed in silence and peace. His revelation encourages us to seek our inner truth, to recognize our own reflection in the greater whole. By learning to observe our inner reflection without disturbing the water, we discover a serenity that transcends the illusions and agitations of the material world.

Ultimately, this parable teaches us that true peace and wisdom lie in the acceptance and contemplation of our true essence. The lake, calm and unruffled, represents the tranquility of the soul that has found its place in the harmony of the universe. It is in this tranquility that we can all reveal the light of our own knowledge and wisdom, reflecting our unique part in the infinite web of existence.

37. The Parrot and the Mantra

Repetition towards reality

In the lush branches of an ancient tree lived a green parrot named Mitra. Unlike the other birds, which sang freely, Mitra had an unusual occupation: reciting the mantra "Om Mani Padme Hum", a gift from a wandering yogi.

At first, the other birds laughed at him, his chirping replaced by a human melody. But Mitra, unwavering, continued his repetition, morning and evening, rain or shine. Days became weeks, weeks became months, and the mantra permeated Mitra's very essence.

One day, as the sun flooded the forest with golden light, Mitra felt a change taking place within him. Each recitation seemed to vibrate his feathers, each syllable pulsed through his being. It was no longer he reciting the mantra, but the mantra expressing itself through him. Constant repetition had carved a deep groove in his heart, and in this groove had blossomed understanding.

It wasn't just the sound of the mantra that was important, but the reality it evoked. "Om Mani Padme Hum" was not a simple phrase, but a key to the deep connection of all things, an opening to the ultimate truth that all is one.

The parrot no longer felt confined to his body or his nature as a bird. He experienced a sense of unity with the trees, the wind, the sky, even the distant stars. Mitra had transcended his form, not by metamorphosing into another creature, but by recognizing his place in the vast richness of the universe.

And then Mitra flew above the canopy, her song transformed. It was no longer the mantra coming from his beak, but a new song, the pure expression of his enlightened existence. The other birds followed, forming a procession behind him, charmed by the melody that seemed to speak to them of their own infinite potential.

The legend of the parrot who had transcended his nature by repeating a sacred mantra spread beyond the forest, inspiring all who heard it. Mitra's story was not one of physical metamorphosis, but of inner transformation, reaching a deeper reality beyond physical appearances and limitations.

Mitra had discovered that repetition was not a mere act of memory, but a path to understanding, and that even the most ordinary creature could achieve extraordinary realization through perseverance and devotion.

The Inner Echo: Path to Realization

Mitra, the mantra-reciting parrot, embodies the essence of transformation through perseverance. His unwavering practice reveals a profound truth: conscious repetition is a gateway to greater understanding. It's not the repetition itself that is transformative, but the intention and attention that accompany it. The mockery of other birds dissipates in the face of the power of Mitra's constancy, teaching us that the ridicule of others must not distract from the personal quest for meaning.

The parrot illustrates that deep devotion can transcend physical appearances and reveal the unified nature of existence. His journey reveals that beyond words, there is a reality that can only be reached through dedicated practice. Mitra thus becomes a symbol of each being's ability to find its place in the universe, not by changing form, but by evolving from within.

Mitra's ascent through the canopy, followed by the others, testifies to the inspiration that a single soul can spread. His inner metamorphosis, shared in a new song, reminds us that every individual, no matter how seemingly simple, carries within him the potential for extraordinary awakening. The legend of Mitra invites us to embrace repetition not as an end in itself, but as a path leading to the full expression of our being.

38. THE DOLPHIN AND THE VAIRAGYA

Joy in renunciation

In the calm waters of the Saraswati River, a young dolphin named Kairava spent his days playing among the waves. His life was a constant dance of leaps and spins, an endless quest for the silver fish that slipped through his teeth like fleeting thoughts. Yet deep inside, Kairava felt a restlessness, a longing for something more, something elusive.

One day, as Kairava was hunting in the bright sunshine, he spotted an old turtle named Vairagini floating effortlessly with an air of profound serenity. Intrigued, Kairava approached her and asked what her secret was.

The old tortoise slowly opened his ancient eyes and said with a voice that sang of time and wisdom: "My dear, I practice vairagya, renunciation. I've learned to free myself from worldly attachments and find joy in simplicity."

Kairava, confused, observed that Vairagini had neither schools of fish to chase nor currents to master. "But without these pleasures, what's left?" he asked.

"Freedom," she replied simply, before plunging into the depths.

The word echoed in Kairava's mind. Freedom. Was it possible to find freedom in renunciation? Driven by a burning curiosity, Kairava decided to try vairagya. Day after day, he resisted the pursuit of silver fish, watched the waves without playing with them, and remained calm even when the wind caressed the water's surface with an invitation to dance.

In time, a strange calm settled over his heart. The desires that had once agitated him seemed less urgent, less crucial. Kairava discovered that every breath could be a pleasure, every heartbeat a rhythm to be celebrated. By giving up his incessant pursuits, he had discovered an ocean of peace surrounding him.

As the moons passed and the seasons changed, Kairava became a symbol of joy and freedom for all beings in the river. Fish swam around him without fear, and even birds stopped to share a moment of tranquility with the dolphin who had given up everything, only to find everything.

Kairava's lesson spread far beyond the clear waters of the Saraswati. The dolphin who had found freedom in renunciation became a story whispered among the reeds and sung by the winds, reminding us all that sometimes, by letting go, we gain what we couldn't grasp by clinging on.

The Undercurrent of Freedom

Kairava the dolphin and his discovery of vairagya teach us that in renunciation lies unexpected freedom. Letting go of incessant desires reveals an undercurrent of peace that runs through existence. This story depicts the profound reality that contentment is not found in the frenetic accumulation of experiences, but in the deep appreciation of the present moment. Kairava's serenity becomes a mirror for those caught up in the whirlwind of the endless pursuit of more and better.

The old Vairagini turtle represents the wisdom that comes with age and experience, showing that true happiness depends not on possessions or external distractions, but on an inner state of being. Vairagini's voluntary simplicity suggests that fulfillment lies in an existence stripped of the superfluous, where joy is drawn from the clarity of an uncluttered mind.

Finally, the story of the dolphin and the tortoise resonates as a hymn to the transformative nature of detachment. It whispers to us that in renouncing worldly attachments, we can find a deeper connection with the universe. Kairava, through her choice to live free from the shackles of covetousness, becomes a beacon of wisdom, reminding us that giving up what we think is indispensable may in fact be the key to unlocking the hidden treasures of existence.

39. The Owl and the Night

Wisdom in the dark

In the village of Dhara, where the shadows stretch long under the weight of the stars, there lived a boy named Arav. His days were filled with sunshine and laughter, but his nights were filled with shadows and terrors. The darkness seemed full of hidden monsters whispering the fears and doubts of the day.

One inky night, when the moon was hidden behind a veil of clouds, Arav met an owl with piercing eyes and a voice as gentle as the night wind. This owl, a sage among sages, was known as Gyanesh, he who sees in the dark.

"Why do you shudder at the darkness, young Arav?" asked Gyanesh, his voice as steady as the roots of a banyan tree.

"The night hides monsters ready to devour my dreams," Arav replied, his voice trembling.

The owl nodded. "What you call monsters are simply illusions, games of light and shadow. Darkness is but a canvas for secret wisdom. Come with me."

Intrigued and trembling with daring, Arav followed Gyanesh into the depths of the night forest. There, the owl led him through a maze of ancient trees to a clearing where the stars seemed to whisper ancient truths.

Gyanesh asked Arav a question, "Look around you. What do you see?"

Arav, his eyes wide open, saw the nocturnal plants blooming in the darkness, the fireflies dancing like sparks of knowledge, and the distant glint of animal eyes sparkling with life.

"There's life... There's beauty," he murmured in wonder.

"Night is simply when another world awakens," Gyanesh explained. "In the darkness, you find creatures that hide during the day. In silence, you hear your own inner voice. Wisdom comes when you learn to see not just with your eyes, but also with your heart and mind."

Every night Arav searched for Gyanesh, and every encounter was a lesson. He learned to recognize the constellations and listen to the language of leaves whispered by the wind. He discovered patience in the stillness of the moon and perseverance in the tireless rhythm of the crickets. In every shadow, he found a story, and in every fear, an opportunity for courage.

As time went by, Arav no longer feared the night. He found a wisdom and peace that transformed him. The boy who dreaded the dark had become a friend of the moon, a seeker of truths hidden in the velvet of night.

And so, Gyanesh's wisdom was realized. For when the daylight receded, Arav now danced with the shadows, understanding that even in the darkest moments, there were sparks of wisdom to be discovered.

Lights of Nocturnal Knowledge

Arav's encounter with the wise owl, Gyanesh, illuminates the idea that darkness is not a veil of terror, but a realm of unexplored wisdom. This story teaches us that fear of the unknown can often obscure our vision of the beauty and truth that lie just beyond our immediate perception. Arav, initially frightened by the darkness, learns to embrace the night as a universe full of life and lessons.

The dialogue between the young boy and the owl highlights the transformative power of understanding. Shadows, once interpreted as threatening, turn out to be manifestations of light, shaping our reality in new and unexpected ways. This realization allows Arav to find beauty where previously there was only fear.

Finally, the story demonstrates that true wisdom requires seeing beyond appearances, using the heart and mind in conjunction with the eyes. The night, with its mysteries and silences, provides the perfect canvas for this inner quest. Arav, learning to discern the sparks of wisdom in the darkness, finds peace and knowledge, reminding us that every moment of uncertainty carries with it the possibility of growth and discovery.

40. Mangosteen and Essence

Inner sweetness

In the heart of the ancient kingdom of Madhura, reigned King Virat, famous for his splendor and majesty. He adorned his palace with mirrors and precious stones, convinced that outer beauty and wealth reflected inner greatness.

One day, during a procession through the fragrant lanes of his kingdom, an old man presented him with a basket of mangosteens, their rough purple skin contrasting with the radiance of the royal ornaments. The king scorned them, deeming them unworthy of his court. But the old man insisted, "O Majesty, don't judge the fruit by its rind. Its true essence lies within."

Curious in spite of himself, Virat accepted the fruit, but it wasn't until late at night, alone in his sumptuous apartments, that he tasted the mangosteen. At first bite, the juicy white flesh awakened in him a sweetness he had never known before. The contrast between the fruit's outward appearance and its exquisite flavor hit him hard.

The next day, the king, guided by an unusual impulse, decided to roam his kingdom disguised as a simple merchant, to discover the nature of his subjects. In the bustling markets, he met generous souls living in modest huts, and saw nobility in the eyes of peasants and wisdom on the lips of beggars. The kindness and richness of spirit he encountered contrasted with the facade of his luxurious palace.

These encounters slowly transformed Virat's heart. He realized that, like the mangosteen, true value lies not in outward appearances, but in inner essence. He began to cherish his subjects for their sincerity and kindness, not for their status or wealth.

King Virat, inspired by the humble fruits and the purity he had tasted, ordered that the palace be opened to all. He replaced the mirrors with windows to see the true face of his kingdom, and turned the gardens into gathering places. The palace's precious stones were sold to feed and educate the children of his kingdom.

The story of the king and the mangosteen tree spanned the centuries, reminding generations that true beauty and wealth lie in the inner essence and gentleness of the heart, not in the deceptive brilliance of outward appearances.

The Radiance of Authenticity

King Virat's tasting of the mangosteen is a tasty metaphor revealing that true beauty and value lie not in outward ornamentation, but in inner quality and richness. This teaching guides us to a deeper understanding that appearances can be deceiving, and that true brilliance is often hidden behind a modest façade.

The king's transformation illustrates the power of humility and simplicity. Venturing incognito among his people, Virat discovers treasures of goodness and wisdom in the daily lives of his subjects, a priceless wealth not reflected in the walls of his palace. This realization teaches him that prestige is not measured in material possessions, but in actions and benevolence.

Finally, Virat's story becomes a timeless reminder that leaders must seek to reflect the light of their people, rather than shine with their own brilliance. The awakened king reveals that enlightened leadership is that which values and elevates the inner essence of each individual, and recognizes that in the hearts of his subjects lies the true splendor of his kingdom.

41. The Garland and the Atman

The unity of individuality

In the shimmering heat of an afternoon in the village of Jhalam, a young boy named Arav was walking along the sacred river, his light steps lifting the golden dust of summer. The banks were lined with a mosaic of wildflowers, swaying in the warm breeze. Arav was captivated by the symphony of colors, but it was the singularity of each flower that fascinated him most - no two were alike.

Old Jayan, garland weaver and village sage, watched Arav from his modest stall. With deft hands, he was gathering flowers in an act of creation, binding them together in a dance of harmony. Arav, curious, approached and sat in silence, his eyes wide with wonder.

"Each flower is an atman," Jayan began, without looking up from his work, "a soul with its own essence, its own beauty, its own unique fragrance. But look at this garland, Arav. Alone, a flower carries an isolated splendor. United, it becomes part of a greater beauty, a song of unity."

Arav listened, fascinated, while Jayan picked out a small purple flower. "This one," he said, "could be you. Unique in form and essence. Next to it, I place a red flower, bright and bold - your best friend perhaps. And here, a white one, pure and soothing - your mother, perhaps. Separately, they captivate, but together..."

He left his sentence hanging as the garland took shape beneath his fingers, a spun metaphor of the atman joining the Brahman, the universal soul.

As Jayan spoke, Arav began to understand. The individuals around him, with their laughter and sorrow, their dreams and hopes, were like these flowers - wonderfully distinct, but bound together by something invisible and impalpable.

The completed garland was hung at the entrance to Jayan's hut, an ode to unity, and Arav returned home, his heart light and his mind open. He began to see his family, friends and even strangers as essential parts of a greater whole, each contributing to the richness and diversity of life.

With this revelation, Arav resolved to celebrate the singularity of each soul while recognizing their union in the extraordinary tapestry of existence. He became a young man who sought unity in diversity, symphony in solitude, and love in the freedom of each atman.

Years went by, and Arav, who had become a garland weaver in his own right, would tell every child in the village the story of the garland and the atman, passing on an ancestral wisdom which asserted that although each flower - each soul - was unique, all together they formed the eternal and indivisible Brahman.

Harmony in Diversity

The lesson Arav takes away from his encounter with Jayan is a powerful echo of the philosophy that celebrates uniqueness while embracing unity. Each individual is a flower in the immense garden of existence, distinct and beautiful in its own right, but only together do they reveal the complete and captivating design of life. This awareness engenders an appreciation of individual beauty and a deep respect for each soul's contribution to the whole.

Arav, in becoming a garland weaver, weaves more than flowers; he weaves the understanding that each person is a unique atman, essential to the fabric of Brahman, the universal soul. He teaches us that singularity should not divide, but enrich the collective tapestry, and that recognizing and valuing this diversity leads to a deeper, more cohesive unity.

Passing on this wisdom to subsequent generations perpetuates the conviction that, although we are different, we are inextricably linked. Life, in all its varied splendor, is a hymn to plurality, a garland of souls that together sing the glory of interconnected existence.

42. THE ELEPHANT AND THE DHARMA

The weight of responsibility

In the thick Sundarbans forest, laced with mysteries and ancient whispers, lived an elephant named Gajendra. His stature was imposing and his tusks, sculpted by the trials of time, gleamed under the rays of dawn. Gajendra, renowned for his strength and wisdom, carried on his back not only the goods of his herd, but also the invisible weight of their hopes and fears.

Every day, he worked tirelessly, his huge feet creating trails through the dense forest, his ears floating like sails capturing nature's secret breaths. But the burden of responsibility began to wear on him, bending his strong back and darkening his once mischievous eyes.

It was against this backdrop of uninterrupted toil that a wise man named Vidyadhar appeared. Old and frail, his only luggage was a simple bundle and a carved walking stick. Vidyadhar watched Gajendra, sensing the weight that oppressed the noble creature's soul.

"Why do you bow your head, majestic Gajendra?" he asked in his clear, penetrating voice.

Gajendra slowly raised his eyes, and a gleam of recognition shone in his eyes. "This is the weight of my dharma, sage Vidyadhar. I carry everyone's needs and fears, but who will carry mine?"

Vidyadhar approached and placed his hand on the elephant's thick hide. "My friend, dharma is not a burden to carry but a path to follow. It must flow like river water, effortlessly, without constraint. You who are so great, can you not see that dharma is the balance between giving and receiving, acting and resting?"

Gajendra remained silent, letting the sage's words seep into his mind.

"Look at the trees, Gajendra. They offer shade and shelter without bending under the weight of this gift. They stand tall, drawing their strength from earth and sky. Likewise, you must find your balance between strength and gentleness, duty and compassion for yourself."

Vidyadhar took a handful of earth and let it slip through his fingers before the elephant's eyes. "Let the wind take away what is not essential. Your dharma is your strength, but don't forget that it must also be your joy."

In the days that followed, Gajendra changed. He learned to share his burdens, to rest under the tall banyan trees, to bathe in the clear waters of the river, splashing laughter like pearls in the air. He taught his herd to help each other, to respect each other's limits, to find harmony.

The herd flourished, not only in numbers but in spirit. Gajendra, now free from the crush of weight, carried his responsibilities not as a burden but as a crown of balance and wisdom, his regal step punctuating the ancient pulse of the Sundarbans forest.

And so Gajendra became not only a guide to his flock, but also a living symbol of authentic dharma, a path trodden with grace and dignity, a lesson in balance and right action for all who crossed his majestic path.

The Balance of Duty

Gajendra's journey towards understanding his dharma reveals an essential truth about the nature of responsibility. They must not be burdens that crush the spirit, but rather acts of balance that nourish the soul. As Gajendra learns from the sage Vidyadhar, it's crucial to align one's obligations with the natural rhythms of giving and receiving, action and rest, so that duty becomes a source of joy rather than a cause of exhaustion.

Gajendra's transformation teaches the importance of self-compassion in fulfilling responsibilities. By giving himself time to rest and learning to delegate, he finds the true essence of strength - not in the ability to carry loads alone, but in the wisdom of sharing them. In so doing, he instills in his flock the values of cooperation and mutual support.

Gajendra's example illustrates that true dharma is not a solitary journey, but a harmonious walk alongside others. His story teaches us that every individual, no matter how strong, needs balance to walk with dignity, and that true wisdom lies in the ability to transform duty into an act of personal and collective fulfillment.

Conclusion

The path to Dharma

We have journeyed together through stories imbued with the richness of Hindu thought, from the majestic elephant in the dense forest to the subtlety of the atman, the essence of the soul. Each of the 42 reflections shared in this book was an invitation to explore more deeply the principles that animate existence, to understand the dharma that is unique to each of us.

Through these symbolic stories, where flora and fauna, gods and men, elements and stars are the protagonists, we've sought to offer you not just a read, but a path towards a richer understanding of life. By resonating with the struggles and joys of these mythical characters, you may have felt the universal bond that connects us all in the great fabric of the universe.

Closing this book marks not an end, but the potential beginning of your own introspection and application of the teachings you've found resonant.

Dharma is not just a doctrine; it's an experience, a commitment to balance and justice, harmony with the world around us and with the inner truth that guides our every step. The lessons learned in each chapter are seeds planted, which, with care and attention, can grow to become guides in moments of choice, challenge and celebration.

It is my hope that "The Elephant and Dharma" has been a source of inspiration for you, a window into an ancient wisdom that continues to shine its light on contemporary paths. May the teachings of Krishna, Shiva, Saraswati and so many others remain with you, as silent companions on your journey towards a deeper understanding of your own existence.

Thank you for sharing this journey with me, and I leave you with a heartfelt thought: may you find your way, like the elephant finds its way through the forest, with strength, grace and unshakeable inner peace.

Namaste.

.

THANKS

I would like to express my gratitude to all those who have made this book possible. To the many scholars and authors who have preserved and interpreted Japanese philosophy over the centuries. To the editorial team who carefully crafted every page of this book. And above all, to you, dear readers, for your interest and passion for these stories and this philosophy that has fascinated us for millennia.

Give your honest opinion on Amazon!

Your suggestions and criticisms are invaluable.

They make every reading experience even more satisfying!

Thank you very much for reading my book.

I wish you all the success you deserve!

SOURCE IMAGES

The author and publisher would particularly like to thank the :

www.midjourney.com

Printed in Great Britain
by Amazon